One Year of 5-Minute Family Devotions For Kids, Teens, And Parents

52 Weeks of Faith-Building Activities, Prayer, And Bible Study For Strengthening Family Connections

Biblical Teachings

CONTENTS

ONE BIG FAMILY

This special book was created to help our families grow closer to God and each other. Being a parent myself, I understand the ups and downs of guiding a family's faith journey. My goal is to share what I've learned along the way, so that it can bring light and strength to your family too.

In addition to the book, I warmly invite you to join our online community on Facebook. It's like a big family where we come together, support each other, and share our experiences on our faith journeys. Our Facebook page is a place where we can ask questions, talk about our feelings, and find comfort in knowing we're not alone.

You are the perfect addition to our little online family. Scan the QR code to be taken to the page. See you there

Introduction

Let The Journey Begin...

Welcome to our family devotional time! This is a special time when we can all come together as a family to learn and grow in our faith, learn about God's love, discover timeless wisdom, and build a stronger bond with one another. Whether you're a parent, a sibling, or a grandparent, this book is for everyone. We are all part of the incredible adventure of seeking God's truth together.

The purpose of our family devotional time is twofold: it's a way for us to grow closer as a family and also to grow closer to God. We'll have the opportunity to share our thoughts, ask questions, and support one another. By spending this time together, we hope to strengthen our bond as a family and deepen our relationship with God.

Inside are 52 weeks (one per week of the year, but feel free to complete them at your own pace) worth of devotions. We'll explore stories and lessons from the Bible, as well as real-world examples, that relate to things we experience in our everyday lives, both as a family and individually. We will hear inspiring messages, and engage in meaningful discussions that will allow each of us to share our thoughts, ask questions, and discover new insights. Together, we will uncover valuable life lessons that will shape our character, deepen our understanding of God's plan, and strengthen our relationship with Him.

Remember, family devotional time is not just about learning, but also about connecting with one another. Let's embrace this opportunity to grow closer as a family, support one another, and encourage each other on our spiritual journeys. Together, we can create a safe and open space where everyone's voice is valued, and where we can find comfort, guidance, and joy in our shared faith.

So let's dive in. It's going to be an exciting journey, and we're so glad to have each and every one of you here with us!

1

LOVE

THE FOUNDATION OF FAMILY

"Love one another deeply, from the heart."

- I PETER 1:22

L ove is like a superpower that we all possess. It's what makes your family so unique and special.

Do you remember the story of the Good Samaritan? Jesus shared this story to teach us about love. There was a man who was beaten and left by the side of the road. People passed by, ignoring his pain. But then, a Samaritan—a stranger—came along. He showed love by stopping to help the injured man, taking care of him, and making sure he was safe. The Samaritan showed us that love knows no boundaries—it goes beyond family ties and extends to all people.

Just like the Good Samaritan, our family can be a shining example of love. We can show love by being kind and considerate to one another. Love is not just a feeling; it's an action. It's helping your sibling with their homework, sharing your favorite toy, or simply giving a hug when someone needs it. When we choose to love, our family becomes a safe haven—a place where we feel accepted, valued, and supported.

Prompt: *Reflect on a time when someone in our family showed you an extraordinary act of love. How did it impact your life, and how can we show more love within our family?*

How can we extend love beyond our family, just like the Good Samaritan did? Can you think of someone in need who could benefit from our acts of love and kindness?

Activity: Love Notes: Each family member writes a heartfelt note expressing love and appreciation for another family member, and then secretly leaves it somewhere for them to find, spreading love and warmth throughout the home.

Let us pray... *Dear God, In this sacred moment, we come before You, grateful for the gift of family and the love that binds us together. We acknowledge the challenges we face as a family, but also the incredible joy and fulfillment that comes from fostering a loving home. Help us to deepen our love for one another, to choose kindness and compassion in every interaction. In Your holy name, we pray. Amen.*

2

GRATITUDE

CULTIVATING A THANKFUL HEART

"Give thanks in all circumstances; for this is God's will for you in Christ Jesus."

- I THESSALONIANS 5:18

G ratitude is like a special lens through which we see the world. It helps us appreciate the small things, the big things, and everything in between. Have you ever noticed how magical it feels when you say "thank you" to someone who has done something kind for you, such as cooking you a delicious meal? It's like spreading joy and warmth through your words. Gratitude is what makes your family shine brightly.

The story of Jesus feeding the five thousand teaches us about gratitude. As it goes, one day, a large crowd gathered to listen to Jesus teach. As evening approached, the people became hungry. Jesus took five loaves of bread and two fish, gave thanks to God, and miraculously fed the entire crowd with plenty of leftovers. What an incredible act of gratitude and provision!

Just like in the story, gratitude can fill our hearts and overflow into our actions. When we cultivate a thankful heart, it changes the way we see the world and the way we treat one another. We become more appreciative of the blessings in our lives, big or small. We begin to notice the beauty of nature, the kindness of others, and the love that surrounds us. Gratitude is a secret ingredient that adds flavor to our family dynamics.

Prompts: *Share one thing you are grateful for today and why it is meaningful to you. How does expressing gratitude make you feel?*

How can we cultivate a thankful heart as a family? Can you think of specific actions we can take to show gratitude to God and to one another?

Activity: Gratitude Jar: Create a jar where family members write down things they are grateful for on pieces of paper and regularly take turns reading them aloud, fostering a culture of appreciation and a visual reminder of blessings.

Let us pray... *Dear God, we thank You for the gift of gratitude and the power it holds in our lives. Help us to cultivate thankful hearts and to appreciate the blessings You have bestowed upon us. May gratitude guide our thoughts, words, and actions, bringing us closer to You and to one another. In Jesus' name, we pray. Amen.*

FORGIVENESS

THE POWER OF LETTING GO

"Be kind and compassionate to one another, forgiving each other, just as in Christ God forgave you."

- EPHESIANS 4:32

D o you have the incredible power of forgiveness – the art of letting go and choosing love over resentment? Forgiveness has the ability to heal wounds, mend relationships, and bring peace to our hearts.

I'm sure we can all think of a time when our sibling, or friend, accidentally broke something that belonged to us. Or when you've had a disagreement with a loved one that escalates into hurtful words and actions. It creates a divide in the relationship, causing tension, anger, and sadness.

Following these moments, you have a choice—to hold onto the hurt and stay mad or to extend forgiveness and offer a chance to rebuild the bond between you.

Forgiveness is not always easy, but it's a superpower that lies within each of us. Just as God forgave us through His son Jesus, we too can extend forgiveness to those who have hurt us. When we choose forgiveness, we break free from the chains of anger and resentment, opening the door to reconciliation and healing.

Prompts: *Can you think of a time when you felt hurt or wronged by someone? Perhaps you were the one who did it? How did forgiveness play a role in resolving the situation?*

Why do you think forgiveness is important in our family? How can we practice forgiveness in our daily lives?

Activity: Forgiveness Rock: Have each family member find a small rock and decorate it with the name of someone they need to forgive or seek forgiveness from, symbolizing the act of letting go and fostering reconciliation.

Let us pray... *Dear God, thank You for showing us the power of forgiveness through Your boundless love. Help us to embrace the gift of forgiveness and let go of any grudges or hurts that weigh us down. Grant us the strength and wisdom to extend forgiveness to one another, just as You have forgiven us. May forgiveness be the foundation of our family, fostering love, healing, and reconciliation. Amen.*

KINDNESS

SPREADING JOY THROUGH SMALL ACTS

"Do not withhold good from those to whom it is due, when it is in your power to act."

- PROVERBS 3:27 (NIV)

K indness is like a ripple in a pond—it starts small but has the power to create waves of happiness and warmth and make a positive impact on those around us.

Just as Christ's love fills our hearts, we can let that love overflow and touch the lives of others through simple acts of kindness. It's the little things that make a big difference—holding the door for someone, offering a helping hand, or giving a compliment. These small acts create a domino effect, inspiring others to pay it forward and spread kindness in their own unique ways.

As a family, you could dedicate one day each week or month to performing acts of kindness for others. Brainstorm together and come up with ideas such as baking cookies for their neighbors, writing heartfelt thank-you notes to your teachers, or donating toys to a local charity. As you engage in these acts of kindness, you'll witness the joy and gratitude you bring to others, and it will fill your own hearts with a deep sense of fulfillment and happiness.

Prompts: *Can you recall a time when someone's kindness made a significant impact on your life? How did it make you feel, and how did it inspire you to spread kindness to others?*

How can we incorporate acts of kindness into our family's daily routine? What are some simple ways we can bring joy to others through our actions?

Activity: Kindness Challenge: Create a family kindness challenge where each member is assigned a random act of kindness to perform for someone else in the family, nurturing a culture of kindness, empathy, and selflessness.

Let us pray... *Dear God, thank You for showing us the power of kindness through Your love and compassion. Help us to be aware of the opportunities around us to spread joy through small acts of kindness. May our actions reflect Your love and bring warmth and happiness to those we encounter. Guide us to be a beacon of kindness in our family, community, and beyond. In Jesus' name, we pray. Amen.*

———◄◊►———

PATIENCE

NURTURING UNDERSTANDING AND EMPATHY

"Be completely humble and gentle; be patient, bearing with one another in love."

- EPHESIANS 4:2

P atience is like a gentle breeze that calms the storms of frustration and brings a sense of peace and harmony. Someone who mastered this was Joseph.

Joseph was a young man who experienced many challenges and hardships in his life. His brothers were jealous of him and sold him as a slave. Yet, even in the face of betrayal and adversity, Joseph remained patient, trusting in God's plan. Eventually, his patience paid off, and he became a powerful leader in Egypt, reuniting with his family and extending forgiveness.

Joseph's story teaches us the importance of patience in nurturing understanding and empathy. When we practice patience, we create space for compassion and empathy to grow. Instead of rushing to judgment or becoming frustrated with one another, we strive to understand each other's perspectives and extend grace. Patience allows us to see beyond the surface and delve into the depths of each other's hearts, fostering a deeper connection and fostering an atmosphere of love and understanding.

In our own family, there have been times when patience has been tested. One particular memory that comes to mind is a family road trip we took. We encountered traffic, detours, and unexpected delays. It was easy to become impatient and let frustration take over. However, we reminded ourselves of the importance of patience. We played games, sang songs, and shared laughter along the way. We chose to see the journey as an opportunity to bond as a family rather than focusing solely on the destination. Our patience not only brought us closer together but also taught us valuable lessons about empathy and understanding.

Prompts: *Can you think of a time when you had to practice patience with someone in your family or a friend? How did patience help you understand them better?*

How can we cultivate patience in our daily lives and encourage empathy toward one another? What are some practical ways we can support and uplift each other?

Activity: Patience Puzzles: Solve puzzles or engage in activities that require patience, such as a jigsaw puzzle or a challenging board game, promoting perseverance, teamwork, and the development of patience skills.

Let us pray... *Dear God, thank You for the gift of patience and the lessons we learn through challenging experiences. Help us to cultivate patience in our family, especially during moments that test our endurance. Teach us to understand and support one another, even when things don't go as planned. May our patience strengthen our bond and reflect Your love in our lives. Amen.*

TRUST

BUILDING STRONG BONDS WITHIN YOUR FAMILY

"Trust in the Lord with all your heart, and do not lean on your own understanding."

- PROVERBS 3:5

Trusting someone requires a leap of faith, a belief that they have our best interests at heart. In a family, trust is the cornerstone that builds strong bonds. It's about relying on each other, knowing that you can count on your loved ones no matter what.

Think of a time when you were learning how to ride a bike. You were filled with excitement and a bit of fear. But as you balanced on those two wheels for the first time, someone special was there, holding the back of your seat, assuring you that they wouldn't let you fall.

Trusting each other means being open and honest, listening without judgment, and offering unwavering support when it's needed. It means being reliable and following through on our promises. When we trust one another, we create an environment where love and respect can thrive.

Just as you trusted them during that bike ride, we are called to trust in the Lord with all our hearts. He is our loving Heavenly Father, always present to guide and protect us. When we trust God, we build a foundation of faith that not only strengthens our bond with Him but also strengthens the bonds within our family.

Prompts: *How does trust contribute to the strength of our family bond? Can you think of specific examples when trust has made a difference in our relationships?*

What are some practical ways we can build and maintain trust within our family? How can we demonstrate trustworthiness and reliability in our words and actions.

Activity: Trust Fall: Take turns practicing the trust fall exercise, where family members stand behind and catch one another, symbolizing the importance of trust and building strong bonds within the family.

Let us pray... *Dear God, thank You for the gift of trust and the opportunity to build strong bonds within our family. Help us to trust in You with all our hearts, knowing that You are always faithful. Guide us in cultivating trust within our family, nurturing an environment where love, respect, and support flourish. Teach us to be trustworthy and reliable, reflecting Your trustworthiness in our relationships. Amen.*

RESPECT

HONORING ONE ANOTHER'S WORTH

"So in everything, do to others what you would have them do to you."

- MATTHEW 7:12

R espect is a powerful word that carries great meaning. It's about recognizing and honoring the worth of every person, including the members of our own family. In a world where we all have many differences, respect becomes the bridge that connects us, reminding us of our shared humanity.

Just as we desire respect from others, we are called to treat others with the same respect we wish to receive. This is beautifully summed up in the Golden Rule, as shared by Jesus in the Bible. When we do to others what we would have them do to us, we foster an atmosphere of mutual respect and kindness within our family.

Respecting one another means practicing active listening, seeking to understand rather than simply responding, even if their views differ from our own. It means speaking with kindness and using words that build up, rather than tear down. It means appreciating the unique qualities and talents that each family member brings to the table.

Respect also involves setting boundaries and honoring the personal space and feelings of one another. It means considering each other's needs and treating each person with fairness and equality.

As a family, let's commit to practicing respect in our daily interactions.

Prompts: *How can we demonstrate respect for each other's feelings, opinions, and boundaries within our family?*

Can you think of a time when someone showed you great respect? How did it make you feel? How can we show that same level of respect to others?

Activity: Respectful Listening: Engage in a dedicated family discussion where each member takes turns talking about someone they respect and why. During this the others practice active and respectful listening, fostering a culture of honoring one another's worth.

Let us pray... *Dear God, we thank You for teaching us the importance of respect in our family relationships. Help us to honor one another's worth and treat each other with kindness, fairness, and equality. Guide our words and actions, so that they may reflect the respect we have for one another. May our family be a place where love and respect flourish, strengthening the bonds that hold us together. In Jesus' name, we pray. Amen.*

UNITY

WORKING TOGETHER AS A TEAM

"How good and pleasant it is when God's people live together in unity!"

- PSALM 133:1

U nity is like a symphony of harmonious voices coming together as one. It's about working together as a team, where each family member plays an important role to create a bond that cannot be easily broken. When we embrace unity within our family, we experience the joy and strength that comes from being united.

One of the greatest examples of unity in the Bible is the story of Noah and the Ark. God instructed Noah to build an enormous ark and gather a diverse array of animals to save them from the great flood. Despite the challenges, Noah and his family worked together in unity, fulfilling God's plan. They collaborated, supported one another, and faced the unknown with faith.

In our own lives, unity is just as crucial. It means recognizing that we are stronger together than we are apart. It means putting aside personal differences and focusing on a shared purpose—the well-being and growth of our family. Unity allows us to overcome obstacles, face challenges, and celebrate victories as a team.

Unity also involves forgiveness and grace. It means recognizing that we all make mistakes and choosing to extend understanding and compassion to one another.

Prompts: *What is your role within the family? How can we work together more effectively as a team within our family?*

Share a time when we felt the strongest sense of unity as a family. What made that experience special, and how can we recreate it in our everyday lives?

Activity: Family Mural: Create a large mural together as a family, where each member contributes by painting or drawing a symbol or image that represents their unique personality and interests. Display the finished mural in a common area, symbolizing unity and diversity within the family. This will highlight the value of working together as a united family.

Let us pray... *Dear God, thank You for the gift of family and the strength that comes from unity. Help us to work together as a team, embracing our differences and focusing on a shared purpose. Guide our words and actions, so that they may promote love, understanding, and cooperation. May our family be a shining example of unity, bringing joy and strength to one another and those around us. Amen.*

COURAGE

FACING CHALLENGES WITH FAITH

"Have I not commanded you? Be strong and courageous. Do not be afraid; do not be discouraged, for the Lord your God will be with you wherever you go. "

- JOSHUA 1:9 (NIV)

C ourage is like a flickering flame that burns bright within us, empowering us to face challenges with faith. It's the inner strength that allows us to step out of our comfort zones and trust in God's guidance. In the face of uncertainty and fear, courage gives us the confidence to press forward, knowing that we are not alone.

One of the remarkable stories of courage in the Bible is the story of David and Goliath. David, a young shepherd boy, faced a giant warrior named Goliath. Though the odds were against him, David did not waver in his faith. With a small stone and unwavering trust in God, he defeated Goliath, showcasing the power of courage rooted in faith.

In our own lives, we encounter challenges that may seem insurmountable. It could be starting a new school, facing a difficult decision, or standing up for what is right. Yet, God calls us to be courageous, knowing that He is by our side every step of the way.

When we face challenges with faith, we trust that God has equipped us with the strength and resilience to overcome them. It means acknowledging our fears but not allowing them to paralyze us. Instead, we draw upon our faith and rely on God's promises, knowing that He will provide us with the courage we need.

Prompts: *Share a time when you felt afraid or challenged. How did you find the courage to face that situation?*

How can we support and encourage one another to be courageous in our daily lives?

Activity: Obstacle Course Challenge: Set up an obstacle course in your backyard or living room using various objects and challenges. As a family, take turns navigating the course, encouraging and supporting each other to face the obstacles with courage and determination.

Let us pray... *Dear God, thank You for being our source of courage and strength. Help us to face challenges with unwavering faith, knowing that You are always with us. When fear tries to hold us back, remind us of Your promises and give us the courage to press forward. Guide our family, so that we may encourage and support one another in times of challenge. Amen.*

10

---●◇●---

HOPE

FINDING STRENGTH IN UNCERTAIN TIMES

"May the God of hope fill you with all joy and peace as you trust in him, so that you may overflow with hope by the power of the Holy Spirit."

- ROMANS 15:13

Life is filled with uncertainties. We face challenges, unexpected twists, and moments of doubt. It's during these times that hope becomes our guiding light, leading us through the darkness and uncertainty. In the Bible, God reminds us that He has plans for us, plans that are filled with hope and a future.

Think about a time when your family faced uncertainty together. It could have been a difficult season, a challenging decision, or an unexpected change. In those moments, hope was what kept you going. It was the belief that things would get better, that there was a purpose behind the struggle, and that God was working things out for your good.

Hope is like a beacon of light that shines through the darkest moments of our lives, giving us strength and assurance. It reminds us that there is always a purpose in our trials and that God is working all things together for our good.

Prompts: *Share a time when you felt uncertain or hopeless as a family. How did you find strength and hope during that time?*

How can we actively cultivate hope in our family? What practical steps can we take to encourage one another and remind ourselves of God's faithfulness?

Activity: Jar of Hope: Decorate a jar and have each family member write down hopes and dreams for the future on colorful slips of paper, placing them in the jar as a reminder of finding strength and inspiration in uncertain times. Choose a length of time to keep it shut and open it back up after it has passed. E.g. 6 months, 1 year, or more.

Let us pray... *Dear God, thank You for the hope we have in you. Help us to trust in your plans and find strength in uncertain times. Fill our hearts with hope, reminding us that you are with us every step of the way. May our family be a beacon of hope to others, shining your light in the darkness. In Jesus' name, we pray. Amen.*

GENEROSITY

SHARING BLESSINGS WITH OTHERS

"And do not forget to do good and to share with others, for with such sacrifices God is pleased."

- HEBREWS 13:16

G enerosity is a beautiful quality that brings joy and blessings to both the giver and the receiver. In the Bible, we are encouraged to do good and share with others. When we share our blessings, whether they are material possessions, time, or acts of kindness, we reflect the love and generosity of God.

Generosity is more than just giving—it's an expression of love, compassion, and selflessness. It's about recognizing the needs of others and responding with kindness and generosity. As a family, you can cultivate a spirit of generosity by looking for opportunities to bless and serve others.

Think about a time when your family demonstrated generosity together. It could be a moment when you donated clothes or toys to those in need, volunteered at a local charity, or offered a helping hand to a neighbor.

These acts of generosity not only made a difference in the lives of others but, I'm sure, also brought a sense of fulfillment and joy to your family.

Prompts: *Share a time when you experienced the joy of generosity. How did it impact both the giver and the receiver?*

How can we continue to cultivate a spirit of generosity in our family? What are some practical ways we can share our blessings with others?

Activity: Blessing Bags: Assemble care packages with essential items and distribute them to those in need, instilling the spirit of generosity and sharing blessings with others.

Let us pray... *Dear God, thank You for the blessings you have given us. Help us to have generous hearts and be willing to share with others. Show us opportunities to bless and serve those in need. May our acts of generosity reflect your love and bring joy to others. In Jesus' name, we pray. Amen.*

HUMILITY

RECOGNIZING OUR STRENGTHS AND WEAKNESSES

"Do nothing out of selfish ambition or vain conceit. Rather, in humility value others above yourselves."

- PHILIPPIANS 2:3

H umility is a virtue that allows us to see ourselves and others with honesty and grace. It's about recognizing our strengths and weaknesses and acknowledging that we are all uniquely created by God.

Do you remember the parable of the Pharisee and the tax collector? Jesus shared this story to illustrate the difference between pride and humility. The Pharisee boasted about his righteousness and looked down on others, while the tax collector humbly recognized his own sinfulness and asked God for mercy. Jesus praised the tax collector's humility and reminded us that those who exalt themselves will be humbled, but those who humble themselves will be exalted.

Humility is not about thinking less of ourselves but thinking of ourselves less. It's about valuing others above ourselves and showing respect and kindness to everyone we encounter.

Reflect on a time when your family encountered a situation that required humility. It could be a moment when someone admitted their mistake, apologized, or asked for forgiveness. Humility allows us to recognize our imperfections, learn from our mistakes, and grow closer as a family.

Prompts: *Share a time when humility played a role in resolving a conflict or strengthening your relationships as a family or in a friendship.*

How can we cultivate a spirit of humility in our family? What are some practical ways we can recognize our strengths and weaknesses and value others above ourselves?

Activity: Strengths and Weaknesses Reflection: Have family members share their strengths and weaknesses, emphasizing the importance of recognizing and appreciating both to cultivate humility and self-awareness.

Let us pray... *Dear God, thank You for creating us with unique strengths and weaknesses. Help us to recognize our limitations and value others above ourselves. Teach us humility and grant us the grace to admit our mistakes and learn from them. May our family be a place where humility thrives, and love abounds. Amen.*

JOY

EMBRACING HAPPINESS IN EVERYDAY MOMENTS

"This is the day that the Lord has made; let us rejoice and be glad in it."

- PSALM 118:24

J oy is a gift from God that can brighten even the simplest moments of our lives. It's about finding happiness and contentment in the everyday things we often take for granted. In the Bible, we are encouraged to rejoice and be glad, recognizing that each day is a precious opportunity to experience God's goodness.

Remember the story of Mary and Martha in the Bible? Jesus visited their home, and while Martha was busy with preparations, Mary sat at Jesus' feet, listening to his teachings. Martha became frustrated and asked Jesus to tell Mary to help her. Jesus responded, "Martha, Martha, you are worried and upset about many things, but few things are needed—or indeed only one. Mary has chosen what is better, and it will not be taken away from her." Mary chose to embrace the moment and find joy in Jesus' presence.

As a family, you can choose to embrace joy in everyday moments. It could be something as simple as sharing a meal together, playing a game, or taking a walk in nature. Look for opportunities to appreciate the beauty around you and express gratitude for the blessings in your lives. When we intentionally seek joy, we find it in unexpected places.

Think about a time when your family experienced pure joy together. It could be a moment of laughter, a shared accomplishment, or simply enjoying each other's company. Joy is contagious, and when we embrace it, it spreads like wildfire, filling our hearts and lifting our spirits.

Prompts: *Share a recent moment of joy that you experienced as a family. How did it make you feel, and why was it special?*

How can we cultivate a spirit of joy in our everyday lives? What are some practical ways we can embrace happiness and gratitude as a family?

Activity: Gratitude Collage: Create a family collage using pictures, drawings, and words that represent moments of joy and happiness, celebrating and embracing joy in everyday moments.

Let us pray... *Dear God, thank You for the gift of joy that fills our hearts. Help us to embrace happiness in everyday moments and find reasons to rejoice. May our family be a source of joy for one another and those around us. Amen.*

14

---◆◇◆---

COMPASSION

SHOWING EMPATHY AND UNDERSTANDING

"Be kind and compassionate to one another, forgiving each other, just as in Christ God forgave you."

- EPHESIANS 4:32

C ompassion is a beautiful expression of love that extends beyond ourselves. It's about showing empathy and understanding to others, putting ourselves in their shoes, and offering a helping hand. In the Bible, we are called to be kind and compassionate, just as God has shown us kindness and forgiveness through Jesus.

Compassion is not just a feeling; it's an action. It's about recognizing the struggles and pain of others and responding with kindness and understanding. It's about being present, listening without judgment, and offering a helping hand when needed.

Imagine this: You're walking home from school one rainy afternoon, feeling down because you had a rough day. The rain is pouring, and you forgot your umbrella. As you trudge along, trying to shield yourself from the rain, you notice a stranger approaching with an umbrella. They see you struggling and kindly offer to share their umbrella with you.

In that simple act of compassion, that stranger showed empathy and understanding. They recognized that you were in need, and without hesitation, they extended their kindness to help you. In that moment, their small gesture brought warmth to your heart and brightened your day.

We've all experienced moments like these, where someone's compassion has touched us deeply. It could be a friend who stayed by your side during a difficult time, a sibling who comforted you when you were upset, or a neighbor who offered support when you were going through a challenging situation. These acts of compassion remind us of the goodness in people and the power of empathy.

Prompts: *Share a time when you showed compassion to someone else. How did it make you feel, and what impact did it have on the person you helped?*

How can we practice compassion in our daily lives? Discuss practical ways to show empathy and understanding towards others, both within and outside of our family.

Activity: Random Acts of Kindness: Each family member selects a day of the week as their 'Kindness Day.' On their designated day, they perform a random act of kindness for someone outside the family, such as a neighbor, friend, or stranger. During a family gathering, share the experiences and reflect on the impact of practicing compassion in the world.

Let us pray... *Dear God, thank You for showing us compassion and teaching us to be kind to others. Help us to have empathetic hearts and extend understanding to those in need. May our family be a source of love and support, shining your light through acts of compassion. In Jesus' name, we pray. Amen.*

PERSEVERANCE

OVERCOMING OBSTACLES THROUGH DETERMINATION

"Let us not become weary in doing good, for at the proper time we will reap a harvest if we do not give up."

- GALATIANS 6:9

Have you ever faced a challenge that seemed too difficult to overcome? Maybe it was a school project that required a lot of time and effort, or a sports activity that pushed you to your limits. In those moments, perseverance becomes our greatest ally.

Perseverance is all about staying determined and pushing forward, even when things get tough. It's having the courage to face obstacles head-on and the resilience to keep going until the end, even when it feels like giving up is the easier option.

In the Bible, the apostle Paul writes to the Galatians, encouraging them not to become weary in doing good. This verse reminds us that our efforts and perseverance will bear fruit in due time. It's a powerful reminder that when we persist and stay committed, we can achieve great things.

Perseverance teaches us valuable life lessons. It teaches us resilience and instills in us the belief that we are capable of overcoming challenges. It develops our character and builds our confidence. It shows us that with determination, patience, and a positive mindset, we can accomplish great things.

Remember, perseverance is not about achieving perfection or never encountering difficulties. It's about embracing the journey, learning from setbacks, and growing stronger in the process. With God's help and the support of one another, you can overcome any obstacle.

Prompts: *Share a time when you faced a challenge and had to persevere. How did you stay determined, and what did you learn from the experience?*

What are some ways we can support each other in overcoming obstacles and staying determined as a family?

Activity: Planting and Nurturing: Choose a plant or a small garden project and assign family members the responsibility of nurturing it from seed to maturity. This challenge requires patience, consistent care, and perseverance as they observe the plant's growth over time.

Let us pray... *Dear God, thank You for being with us in times of challenge and helping us develop perseverance. Give us the strength and determination to overcome obstacles and never give up. Help us trust in Your guidance and believe in our own abilities. In Jesus' name, we pray. Amen.*

16

HONESTY

BUILDING TRUST THROUGH TRUTHFULNESS

"The Lord detests lying lips, but he delights in people who are trustworthy."

- PROVERBS 12:22

Honesty is like a strong foundation that builds trust within our families. When we are honest with one another, we create an environment of openness, respect, and authenticity. Being truthful is not always easy, but it is an essential quality that strengthens our relationships.

In the book of Proverbs, we are reminded that the Lord detests lying lips, but He delights in people who are trustworthy. God values honesty because it reflects His character and fosters healthy connections between individuals. When we choose to be honest, we align ourselves with His truth.

Within our families, honesty plays a crucial role in building trust. When we speak the truth, even if it's difficult or uncomfortable, we show our loved ones that they can rely on us. Trust is the cornerstone of strong relationships, and it grows when we consistently demonstrate honesty in our words and actions.

Being honest also means taking responsibility for our mistakes. It's about admitting when we are wrong, seeking forgiveness, and working towards making things right. This level of vulnerability and humility fosters an environment of grace and understanding within our families.

Prompts: *Share a time when you faced a difficult situation where honesty played a crucial role. How did honesty strengthen your relationships?*

How can we practice honesty in our everyday lives, both within our family and in our interactions with others?

Activity: Honesty Box: Place a box in a central location in the house where family members can anonymously share their honest thoughts, feelings, or concerns. Set a regular time to discuss the contents of the box as a family, fostering open and trusting communication.

Let us pray... *Dear God, thank You for the value You place on honesty and truthfulness. Help us cultivate a spirit of honesty within our family, where trust is built and relationships are strengthened. Grant us the courage to speak the truth in love, even when it is difficult. May our words and actions reflect Your truth and grace. Amen.*

FRIENDSHIP

CELEBRATING THE GIFT OF COMPANIONSHIP

"A friend loves at all times, and a brother is born for a time of adversity."

- PROVERBS 17:17

F riendship is a precious gift from God that brings joy, support, and companionship into our lives. When we have true friends, we are blessed with someone who loves us, understands us, and stands by us through all seasons of life.

In the book of Proverbs, we are reminded that a friend loves at all times. True friendship goes beyond just having fun together; it's about being there for one another through the highs and lows. Friends celebrate our victories, lend a listening ear during challenging times, and offer a shoulder to lean on when we need it most.

Within our families, the bond of friendship plays a vital role. Siblings can be each other's best friends, and parents can foster a deep sense of friendship with their children. When we cultivate friendship within our family unit, we create an atmosphere of trust, understanding, and unconditional love.

Friendship requires effort and intentionality. It's about being present, listening attentively, and offering support. It's about celebrating each other's strengths and accepting one another's flaws. It's about showing kindness, forgiveness, and compassion in our interactions.

Let us treasure the gift of friendship and celebrate the companionship we have with one another. May we strive to be true friends who love, support, and bring joy to those around us. And above all, may we always cherish the friendship we have with Jesus, our constant companion.

Prompts: *Share a special memory of a time when a friend provided support or brought joy into your life. How did that friendship impact you?*

How can we nurture friendship within our family? What are some practical ways we can show love and support to one another?

Activity: Friendship Appreciation Day: Dedicate a day for celebrating friendship by inviting each family member to invite one or more friends over for a special gathering or BBQ. Engage in activities that promote bonding, such as playing games, sharing stories, and expressing gratitude for the friendships shared. Reflect on the importance and impact of friendship in our lives.

Let us pray... *Dear God, thank You for the precious gift of friendship. Help us value and nurture the friendships we have within our family. Teach us to be true friends, loving and supporting one another through all seasons of life. And may we always cherish the friendship we have in Jesus. In His name, we pray. Amen.*

18

CONTENTMENT

FINDING FULFILLMENT IN WHAT WE HAVE

"Keep your lives free from the love of money and be content with what you have, because God has said, 'Never will I leave you; never will I forsake you.'"

- HEBREWS 13:5

In a world that constantly tells us we need more to be happy, contentment can feel like a distant goal. We are bombarded with messages that fuel our desires and make us believe that true fulfillment lies in acquiring more possessions, achieving greater success, or keeping up with others. But the truth is, contentment cannot be found in material things or external circumstances.

Contentment is a state of the heart, a mindset that transcends the ups and downs of life. It is finding fulfillment and gratitude in what we already have, rather than longing for what we lack. It is about recognizing the blessings that surround us and cultivating a spirit of thankfulness.

The Bible reminds us to keep our lives free from the love of money and to be content with what we have. God assures us that He will never leave us or forsake us. This promise reassures us that our ultimate source of fulfillment and security is found in our relationship with Him, not in material possessions.

As a family, we can embrace contentment by shifting our focus from what we don't have to what we do have. We can practice gratitude by expressing appreciation for the simple joys and blessings that often go unnoticed. Contentment enables us to live with a sense of peace, joy, and satisfaction, even in the midst of challenges or when faced with unmet desires.

Prompts: *What are some things we are grateful for as a family? How can we practice contentment and express gratitude for these blessings?*

How can we avoid falling into the trap of always wanting more? How can we find fulfillment in experiences, relationships, and the intangible things that money can't buy?

Activity: Gratitude Scavenger Hunt: Create a scavenger hunt where family members search for and document things they are grateful for within their home or community, fostering a sense of contentment and appreciation for what they have.

Let us pray... *Dear God, thank You for the blessings in our lives. Help us find contentment and fulfillment in what we have, rather than always desiring more. Teach us to be grateful and appreciate the simple joys and blessings that come from You. May our family be characterized by a spirit of contentment and gratitude. In Jesus' name, we pray. Amen.*

19

RESPONSIBILITY

TAKING OWNERSHIP OF OUR ACTIONS

"So then, each of us will give an account of ourselves to God."

- ROMANS 14:12

Responsibility is an important virtue that helps us navigate through life with integrity and accountability. It means taking ownership of our words, choices, and actions, and recognizing the impact they have on ourselves and others. As a family, embracing responsibility creates a foundation of trust and respect within our household.

Responsibility starts with self-awareness and self-reflection. It involves being honest with ourselves and acknowledging when we make mistakes or fall short. Rather than making excuses or blaming others, taking responsibility means admitting our faults, seeking forgiveness, and learning from our experiences.

Do you remember the tax collector we spoke about earlier? His name was Zacchaeus. He was a tax collector who was known for his dishonest practices and for taking advantage of others. One day, Zacchaeus heard that Jesus was passing through his town, and he was curious to see Him.

Zacchaeus was a short man, and as the crowd gathered to see Jesus, he couldn't see over their heads. So, he climbed a sycamore tree to get a better view. When Jesus reached that spot, He looked up and called Zacchaeus by name. Jesus told him that He wanted to come to his house.

This encounter with Jesus changed Zacchaeus' life. In the presence of Jesus, Zacchaeus felt convicted of his wrongdoings. He realized the weight of his dishonest actions and the hurt he had caused to others. Zacchaeus took responsibility for his past actions and declared to Jesus and the crowd, "Look, Lord! Here and now I give half of my possessions to the poor, and if I have cheated anybody out of anything, I will pay back four times the amount."

Zacchaeus' response demonstrates a genuine heart of repentance and responsibility. He didn't make excuses or try to justify his actions. Instead, he took immediate steps to make amends and make things right. Jesus acknowledged Zacchaeus' repentance and declared that salvation had come to his house that day.

Through this story, we learn the importance of taking responsibility for our actions. Zacchaeus teaches us that it's never too late to change, to seek forgiveness, and to make amends. Just like Zacchaeus, we can experience the transformative power of Jesus' love and find rest for our weary souls when we choose to take responsibility and turn to Him.

Prompts: *Can you think of a time when you took responsibility for your actions? How did it make you feel, and what were the outcomes?*

In what ways can we demonstrate responsibility in our family relationships and interactions with others?

Activity: Family Chore Chart: Create a chore chart that assigns age-appropriate responsibilities to each family member. Discuss the importance of taking ownership of our actions and working together to maintain a clean and organized household.

Let us pray... *Dear God, thank You for the story of Zacchaeus, who showed us the power of taking responsibility for our actions. Help us to have a repentant heart and the courage to make things right when we have done wrong. Teach us to be responsible in our relationships and to seek restoration and reconciliation. We trust in Your love and grace to guide us on this journey. In Jesus' name, we pray. Amen.*

20

INTEGRITY

LIVING WITH MORAL CHARACTER AND HONESTY

"The integrity of the upright guides them, but the unfaithful are destroyed by their duplicity."

- PROVERBS 11:3

Integrity is like a compass that guides us in making decisions and living a life of moral character and honesty. It's about being true to ourselves and others, even when no one is watching. Let's explore the importance of integrity through a relatable story.

Imagine a young boy named Ethan who loved playing soccer. He was known for his skills on the field, but one day during an important match, something unexpected happened. As the ball rolled towards him, Ethan accidentally touched it with his hand, resulting in a penalty. The referee didn't see it, and none of his teammates noticed. Ethan faced a choice: Should he keep quiet and gain an advantage for his team, or should he admit his mistake and show integrity?

In that moment, Ethan's moral compass guided him. He knew deep down that honesty and integrity mattered more than winning the game.

He raised his hand, called the referee's attention, and confessed his error. The opposing team was awarded a penalty kick, and Ethan's team lost the match. However, Ethan gained something much more valuable—he gained respect and trust from his teammates, coaches, and even the opposing team.

Integrity is about doing the right thing, even when it's challenging or may come at a personal cost. It's about being honest and living in a way that aligns with our values and beliefs. When we choose integrity, we build a foundation of trust and respect in our relationships, and our character shines brightly.

Just as Ethan's integrity impacted his soccer team, our integrity affects our families and communities. When we live with moral character and honesty, we become role models for those around us. We inspire others to make similar choices and create a culture of integrity in our families and beyond.

Prompts: *Can you think of a time when you were faced with a choice between honesty and dishonesty? How did you handle it, and what were the outcomes?*

In what ways can we practice integrity in our daily lives? How can we encourage each other to make choices that align with our values?

Activity: Integrity Role-Play: Divide the family into pairs and assign each pair a scenario that challenges their integrity. They must act out the scenario, demonstrating how they would respond with moral character and honesty. Engage in a discussion afterward to explore different approaches and reinforce the importance of integrity. E.g. Finding a wallet full of cash that doesn't belong to you.

Let us pray... *Dear God, thank You for teaching us the importance of integrity and living with moral character and honesty. Help us to be people of integrity in all that we do, even when faced with difficult choices. Strengthen us to do what is right, even when it may be challenging. May our lives reflect Your truth and righteousness. Amen.*

21

PRAYER

CONNECTING WITH GOD IN CONVERSATION

"Do not be anxious about anything, but in every situation, by prayer and petition, with thanksgiving, present your requests to God."

- PHILIPPIANS 4:6

P rayer is a powerful tool that connects us with God and deepens our relationship with Him. It is like having a heartfelt conversation with our Heavenly Father, where we can pour out our hearts, seek guidance, find comfort, and express our gratitude. Prayer is an essential part of our spiritual journey, and it brings us closer to God and to one another as a family.

In the Bible, we find numerous examples of the transformative power of prayer. One such story is that of Hannah, a woman who longed for a child. Hannah was burdened with sorrow and poured out her heart to God in fervent prayer at the temple. She prayed with such earnestness and sincerity that her lips moved, but no words were heard. Eli, the priest, observed her and, recognizing her devotion, assured her that God had heard her prayer. In due time, Hannah's prayer was answered, and she became the mother of Samuel, who would grow up to be a great prophet and leader.

Hannah's story teaches us that prayer is not simply reciting words; it is a heartfelt conversation with God. It is an opportunity to bring our deepest desires, fears, and joys before Him, knowing that He hears us. Prayer allows us to seek God's wisdom and guidance, find comfort in His presence, and experience His peace that surpasses all understanding. Just as Hannah's prayers were answered, our prayers, too, have the power to shape our lives and draw us closer to God.

As a family, we can grow the habit of prayer by setting aside dedicated times for family prayer, where we come together to express our gratitude, share our concerns, and lift one another up in prayer.

Prompts: *How has prayer made a difference in your life or in situations you have faced?*

What are some ways we can incorporate prayer into our daily routines as a family?

Activity: Prayer Circle: Sit together in a circle as a family and take turns sharing prayer requests or expressing gratitude. After each person shares, the family collectively prays for that individual's needs or thanksgiving. This activity strengthens the bond with God and each other through heartfelt conversation and prayer.

Let us pray... *Dear God, thank You for the gift of prayer, which allows us to connect with You in conversation. Help us to approach prayer with sincerity, knowing that You hear us and care for us. Teach us to seek Your wisdom, find comfort in Your presence, and experience the joy of knowing You intimately. May prayer be a vital part of our family life, strengthening our faith and drawing us closer to You. Amen.*

22

GRACIOUSNESS

EXTENDING KINDNESS EVEN IN DIFFICULT SITUATIONS

"Therefore, as God's chosen people, holy and dearly loved, clothe yourselves with compassion, kindness, humility, gentleness, and patience."

- COLOSSIANS 3:12

G raciousness is a beautiful virtue that allows us to extend kindness and compassion even in challenging and difficult situations. It is an expression of love, understanding, and forgiveness towards others, even when they may not deserve it. As a family, embracing graciousness creates an atmosphere of peace, harmony, and understanding within our home.

In the Bible, we find guidance and inspiration on graciousness in Colossians 3:12, which says, "Therefore, as God's chosen people, holy and dearly loved, clothe yourselves with compassion, kindness, humility, gentleness, and patience."

This verse reminds us that as God's chosen people, we are called to embody these qualities, including graciousness, in our interactions with others. It serves as a gentle reminder of the importance of treating others with compassion, kindness, and humility, regardless of the circumstances we may face.

As a family, we can practice graciousness by being mindful of our words and actions, especially during times of conflict or disagreement. It is in these difficult moments that we have an opportunity to choose grace over anger, understanding over judgment, and forgiveness over resentment.

Prompts: *Can you think of a time when someone showed you graciousness? How did it impact you?*

How can we extend kindness and understanding even when faced with difficult situations?

Activity: Gracious Acts Challenge: Challenge each family member to identify opportunities for gracious acts throughout the week. These acts can include holding the door for someone, offering a genuine compliment, or assisting a neighbor or community member in need. You should pick 1-3 to focus on for the week and try your best to complete it as much as possible. Share experiences and reflections as a family, fostering a culture of graciousness in everyday life.

Let us pray... *Dear God, thank You for Your boundless grace and mercy. Help us to extend graciousness to others, even when it may be challenging. Teach us to respond with love and understanding, embracing forgiveness and empathy. May our words and actions reflect Your love in every situation. Grant us the strength to choose kindness, especially when faced with adversity. Amen.*

23

WISDOM

SEEKING GUIDANCE IN DECISION-MAKING

"The beginning of wisdom is this: Get wisdom. Though it cost all you have, get understanding."

Wisdom is a precious gift that allows us to make thoughtful and discerning decisions in our lives. It is the ability to apply knowledge, experience, and understanding to navigate through the complexities of life. As a family, embracing wisdom creates a foundation for sound judgment, growth, and learning together.

In the Bible, we are encouraged to seek wisdom in Proverbs 4:7. This verse highlights the importance of valuing wisdom and the pursuit of understanding. It reminds us that wisdom is not something we stumble upon but something we actively seek.

Just like King Solomon, who humbly asked God for wisdom to govern His people, we too can seek God's guidance in every aspect of our lives. Through prayer and reading the Scriptures, we gain insights and discernment that can shape our decisions and actions. Seeking wisdom involves listening to different perspectives, seeking advice from trusted mentors, and being open to learning from our experiences.

As a family, we can cultivate wisdom by fostering an environment of open communication and active listening. We can engage in meaningful conversations, encouraging each family member to share their thoughts and perspectives. By doing so, we gain different insights and broaden our understanding of the world around us.

Prompts: *Can you think of a time when seeking wisdom influenced a decision you made? How did it shape the outcome?*

How can we incorporate seeking God's wisdom in our daily lives and decision-making as a family?

Activity: Family Decision-Making: Engage in a family decision-making process for a significant event or choice. Discuss the value of seeking guidance and wisdom from each other, encouraging thoughtful and wise decision-making.

Let us pray... *Dear Heavenly Father, we thank You for the gift of wisdom. Help us to seek wisdom in all that we do, recognizing that true understanding comes from You. Grant us discernment as we make decisions, both big and small. Guide our thoughts, words, and actions, so that they may be aligned with Your will. May we grow in wisdom together as a family, relying on Your guidance. Amen.*

24

ENCOURAGEMENT

LIFTING EACH OTHER UP WITH WORDS OF SUPPORT

"Therefore encourage one another and build one another up, just as you are doing."

- I THESSALONIANS 5:11

Encouragement is a powerful tool that brings hope, inspiration, and strength to our lives. It is the act of uplifting one another with words of support, kindness, and affirmation. As a family, embracing encouragement creates an atmosphere of love, positivity, and growth within our home.

In the Bible, we are encouraged to "encourage one another and build one another up" in 1 Thessalonians 5:11. This verse reminds us of the importance of using our words to lift each other's spirits. It teaches us that our words have the power to impact others in meaningful ways.

Just like Barnabas, a disciple in the early Christian community, who was known as the "Son of Encouragement," we too can be a source of encouragement to those around us. Barnabas encouraged and supported others, believing in their potential and affirming their worth. His words of encouragement brought hope and inspired others to persevere in their faith.

As a family, we can cultivate a culture of encouragement by intentionally using our words to uplift one another. We can offer praise for achievements, express appreciation for acts of kindness, and provide words of comfort during challenging times. Encouragement goes beyond mere compliments; it involves genuinely recognizing and affirming the unique qualities and strengths of each family member.

Prompts: *Think of a time when someone's words of encouragement made a positive impact on you. How did it make you feel, and how did it influence your actions?*

How can we make encouragement a regular practice within our family? What are some specific ways we can uplift and support one another with our words?

Activity: Positive Affirmation Wall: Create a wall or bulletin board dedicated to positive affirmations and uplifting messages within the family. Encourage family members to write and share words of support and encouragement with each other.

Let us pray... *Dear Heavenly Father, we thank You for the power of encouragement. Help us to be mindful of the words we speak and the impact they have on others. Teach us to uplift and support one another with kindness, affirmation, and words of hope. May our family be a source of encouragement to those around us, spreading positivity and love. Amen.*

25

SERVICE

USING OUR TALENTS TO HELP OTHERS

"Each of you should use whatever gift you have received to serve others, as faithful stewards of God's grace in its various forms."

- 1 PETER 4:10

S ervice is a fundamental aspect of our faith journey as followers of Christ. It reflects the heart of Jesus, who came into this world not to be served, but to serve and give His life as a ransom for many. As a family, we have the opportunity to follow in His footsteps and use our talents to bring hope, love, and support to those around us.

In our everyday lives, we encounter countless opportunities to serve others. It could be as simple as lending a helping hand to a friend in need, comforting someone who is hurting, or using our skills to contribute to a greater cause. When we engage in acts of service, we become vessels of God's love, spreading His light in a world that often needs it the most.

One powerful example of service is when Jesus washed the feet of His disciples. In a powerful act of humility, Jesus took on the role of a servant and washed the feet of His followers. This act not only demonstrated

His love for them but also taught them the importance of serving one another with humility and selflessness.

Ask yourselves, "How can we use our talents and resources to make a positive impact in the lives of those around us?" It may involve volunteering at a local shelter, participating in a community clean-up project, or even supporting a charitable organization that aligns with our values.

Prompts: *What are some talents and skills each family member possesses that can be used to serve others?*

Brainstorm and plan a service project that your family can undertake together. How can you use your gifts and resources to make a positive impact in your community?

Activity: Family Volunteer Day: Plan a day where the entire family volunteers together at a local charity or community organization, using their talents and skills to help others in need, emphasizing the importance of service and compassion.

Let us pray... *Dear Heavenly Father, thank You for the gift of service. Help us to recognize the talents You have entrusted to us and inspire us to use them for the benefit of others. Teach us to be faithful stewards of Your grace and to demonstrate love through acts of service. May our family be a shining example of selflessness and compassion. Amen.*

26

SELF-CONTROL

MANAGING EMOTIONS AND DESIRES

"A person without self-control is like a city with broken-down walls."

- PROVERBS 25:28 (NLT)

S elf-control is an essential virtue that allows us to manage our emotions and desires. It empowers us to make wise choices, resist temptation, and navigate through life's challenges with integrity and discipline.

In the book of Proverbs, we are reminded of the importance of self-control through a powerful analogy. The verse compares a person without self-control to a city with broken-down walls. In ancient times, a city's walls served as a crucial defense against external threats, providing security and protection for its inhabitants. When the walls were intact and well-maintained, the city stood strong and secure. However, if the walls were broken and left in disrepair, the city became vulnerable to attacks, exposing its residents to danger and harm.

Likewise, self-control acts as our internal walls, guarding our hearts and minds against impulsive decisions and destructive behaviors. When we exercise self-control, we strengthen our defenses against harmful influences that seek to derail us from our values and goals. It enables us to resist the temptations that come our way and make choices that align with our principles and beliefs.

Imagine a family without self-control. Like a city with broken walls, their lives are vulnerable to chaos and discord. Emotions may run wild, leading to conflicts and hurtful words. Desires and impulses may dictate actions, resulting in regrettable decisions and strained relationships. However, when self-control is embraced and practiced, the family becomes a haven of peace, where individuals exercise restraint, empathy, and understanding.

Managing our emotions and desires requires intentional effort and practice. It involves recognizing our triggers, understanding our limitations, and developing healthy coping mechanisms. By exercising self-control, we learn to respond to situations with grace, patience, and wisdom.

Prompts: *Share a time when practicing self-control was challenging for you. How did it impact the outcome of the situation?*

Discuss practical ways we can support one another in developing self-control. How can we hold each other accountable?

Activity: Temptation Tower: Set up a tower made of tempting treats (e.g., cookies, candies) in the center of the table. Challenge family members to practice self-control by resisting the temptation to eat the treats. Discuss strategies used and lessons learned about managing desires and practicing self-control.

Let us pray... *Dear Heavenly Father, thank You for the wisdom and guidance found in Your Word. Help us to understand the importance of self-control in our lives and within our family. Grant us the strength and discipline to resist temptation and make choices that honor You. May our hearts and minds be guarded by self-control, allowing us to create a peaceful and loving environment in our home. Amen.*

27

PEACE

CULTIVATING A CALM AND HARMONIOUS ATMOSPHERE

"Let the peace of Christ rule in your hearts, since as members of one body you were called to peace."

- COLOSSIANS 3:15A (NIV)

P eace is a precious gift that brings calmness, harmony, and unity to our lives and relationships. It is a state of tranquility that transcends external circumstances, allowing us to experience inner serenity and contentment. Within our family, peace creates a safe and nurturing environment where love, understanding, and cooperation flourish.

Have you heard of the story of Jesus and the storm? One evening, as Jesus and His disciples were sailing across the Sea of Galilee, a fierce storm arose, threatening to capsize their boat. The disciples were filled with fear and panic, but Jesus, even in the midst of chaos, demonstrated His authority over the storm. With a simple command, He rebuked the winds and the waves, bringing about a great calm.

This miraculous event reveals not only Jesus' power over nature but also

His ability to bring peace to any situation. It reminds us that true peace is not the absence of storms in our lives but the presence of Jesus in the midst of them. Just as Jesus calmed the external storm, He desires to bring peace to the storms that may be raging within us—whether they are conflicts, worries, or anxieties.

In your family, you can grow peace by following Jesus' example. We can choose to respond to challenging situations with a spirit of peace and seek resolution through open communication and understanding. We can practice forgiveness, letting go of grudges, and making up with one another. By extending grace and showing empathy towards one another, we create an atmosphere where peace can thrive.

Prompts: *Share a time when you experienced a sense of peace in a difficult or chaotic situation. How did it impact your outlook and response?*

How can we actively contribute to a peaceful atmosphere within our family? What are some practical steps we can take?

Activity: Mindful Meditation: Set aside a designated time for a family meditation session. Guide the family through a peaceful and calming meditation exercise, emphasizing the importance of cultivating inner peace and harmony.

Let us pray... *Dear Lord, we thank You for the gift of peace that surpasses all understanding. Help us to cultivate peace within our family, allowing Your peace to rule in our hearts. Grant us the wisdom and strength to navigate conflicts with grace and empathy. May our home be a place of tranquility and love, reflecting Your peace to the world around us. Amen.*

28

PERFECTIONISM

EMBRACING IMPERFECTIONS AND LEARNING FROM MISTAKES

"But he said to me, 'My grace is sufficient for you, for my power is made perfect in weakness.' Therefore I will boast all the more gladly about my weaknesses, so that Christ's power may rest on me."

- 2 CORINTHIANS 12:9 (NIV)

Perfectionism is a mindset that often tells us we must strive for flawlessness and achievement in every aspect of our lives. While it's important to have high standards and work diligently, the pursuit of perfection can lead to anxiety, self-doubt, and a constant fear of failure. As a family, we can learn to embrace imperfections, celebrate growth, and find valuable lessons in our mistakes.

In the Bible, we discover that even the most faithful and extraordinary individuals faced moments of imperfection and made mistakes. One such example is the story of Peter, one of Jesus' closest disciples. Peter was known for his boldness and commitment to following Jesus, but he also experienced moments of weakness. One night, when Jesus was arrested, Peter denied knowing Him not just once, but three times. In that moment, Peter's imperfection and fear overwhelmed him.

Yet, what we learn from Peter's story is that imperfections do not define us, nor do they diminish our worth in God's eyes. After His resurrection, Jesus appeared to Peter and offered him forgiveness and restoration. Peter's mistakes became opportunities for growth and deeper understanding. Through his experiences, Peter learned humility, reliance on God's grace, and the importance of extending that same grace to others.

As a family, we can foster an environment where perfectionism is replaced with grace and acceptance. We can celebrate our achievements while also acknowledging our imperfections as opportunities for learning and growth. By encouraging one another to embrace vulnerability and share our mistakes, we create a space where unconditional love and support prevail.

Prompts: *Share a time when you made a mistake or faced a setback. What did you learn from that experience, and how did it contribute to your personal growth?*

How can we support and encourage one another to embrace imperfections and learn from our mistakes?

Activity: Imperfection Celebration: Plan a family gathering where everyone intentionally engages in activities or games that highlight imperfections, such as a "silly talent show" or a "create-a-mess" art session. Emphasize the joy and value in embracing imperfections and learning from mistakes.

Let us pray... *Dear God, thank You for loving us unconditionally and extending Your grace to us, even in our moments of imperfection. Help us to let go of the burden of perfectionism and embrace our flaws and mistakes as opportunities for growth. Teach us to extend grace to one another, just as You have graciously extended it to us. May we find strength and wisdom in You, knowing that Your power is made perfect in our weaknesses. In Jesus' name, we pray. Amen.*

—◆◇◆—

29

FAMILY TRADITIONS

THE VALUE OF SHARED RITUALS AND MEMORIES

*"These commandments that I give you today are to be on your hearts.
Impress them on your children. Talk about them when you sit at home and
when you walk along the road, when you lie down, and when you get up."*

- DEUTERONOMY 6:6-7 (NIV)

F amily traditions are like a thread that weaves through generations, connecting us to our past and grounding us in a sense of belonging. They create lasting memories, strengthen our bonds, and provide a sense of stability and identity. Family traditions can be as simple as a weekly game night or as significant as celebrating holidays in a unique and meaningful way. Whatever form they take, these shared rituals carry great value in our lives.

In the Bible, we see the importance of passing down traditions and teachings from one generation to the next. In the book of Deuteronomy, God commands His people to impress His commandments on their hearts and diligently teach them to their children. He emphasizes the significance of keeping the memory of their faith and heritage alive through continuous conversation and intentional practices. This passage reminds us that family traditions can serve as a vehicle for passing down values, beliefs, and cherished memories.

When we engage in family traditions, we create a sense of continuity and stability that our children can carry with them throughout their lives. These traditions provide an opportunity for us to intentionally connect with one another, share stories and experiences, and build a treasure trove of cherished memories. They can be as simple as cooking a favorite family recipe together, going on an annual vacation, or gathering for a special meal during holidays.

May our family treasure and cultivate meaningful traditions that strengthen our bonds, create lasting memories, and pass down the rich tapestry of our heritage to future generations. May these traditions be a source of joy, love, and unity within our home.

Prompts: *What are some of our favorite family traditions and why do they hold significance for us?*

How can we create new traditions that reflect our values and strengthen our bond as a family?

Activity: Family Memory Jar: Decorate a jar and encourage family members to write down memorable moments or experiences from family traditions and place them in the jar. During special occasions, gather as a family to read and reminisce about the shared rituals and memories.

Let us pray... *Dear God, thank You for the gift of family and the traditions that bring us closer together. Help us to cultivate a sense of shared rituals and memories that will bind us as a family and pass down our values and beliefs to future generations. May our traditions create a sense of belonging, foster love and appreciation for one another, and build a legacy of faith and love. Amen.*

30

RESILIENCE

BOUNCING BACK FROM SETBACKS WITH STRENGTH

"So do not fear, for I am with you; do not be dismayed, for I am your God. I will strengthen you and help you; I will uphold you with my righteous right hand."

— ISAIAH 41:10 (NIV)

Life often presents us with unexpected obstacles and difficulties. In those moments, it's easy to feel overwhelmed and discouraged. But as a family, we have the opportunity to cultivate resilience and face these challenges with strength, knowing that God is with us every step of the way.

In the Bible, we find the story of Daniel as a remarkable example of resilience. Daniel was a young man who faced tremendous adversity when he was taken captive and brought to Babylon. Despite being in a foreign land with different customs and beliefs, Daniel remained steadfast in his faith and commitment to God. He faced countless trials, including being thrown into a den of lions because of his refusal to compromise his beliefs. But through it all, Daniel remained resilient, trusting in God's faithfulness and experiencing His protection and deliverance.

Daniel's story teaches us that resilience is not about avoiding difficult situations but about relying on God's strength and guidance in the midst of them. It is about remaining faithful and standing firm in our convictions, even when faced with opposition or adversity. Just as God was with Daniel, He promises to be with us, strengthening us, helping us, and upholding us with His righteous right hand.

As a family, we can cultivate resilience by encouraging one another, reminding ourselves of God's promises, and seeking His guidance through prayer and studying His Word. We can share stories of individuals who have shown resilience in the face of adversity and discuss the lessons we can learn from their experiences. By anchoring our hearts and minds in God's truth, we can overcome setbacks and challenges, growing in resilience and drawing closer to Him as a family.

Prompts: *How can we rely on God's strength and guidance when faced with challenges?*

Share a time when you witnessed someone showing resilience. What inspired you about their experience?

Activity: Resilience Reflection - Bible Stories and Personal Experiences: Gather as a family and start a conversation about resilience. Begin by sharing favorite Bible stories that highlight resilience, such as the story of Joseph, David and Goliath, or the story of Job. Discuss the challenges faced by the characters in these stories, how they demonstrated resilience, and the lessons that can be learned from their experiences.

Let us pray... *Dear Heavenly Father, thank You for Your promise to be with us and strengthen us in times of difficulty. Teach us to rely on Your guidance and trust in Your faithfulness as we face challenges as a family. Grant us resilience, so that we may stand firm in our faith and find strength in You. May our family grow in resilience, knowing that You are our source of strength and hope. Amen.*

31

COMMUNICATION

LISTENING AND EXPRESSING OURSELVES EFFECTIVELY

"Let your conversation be always full of grace, seasoned with salt, so that you may know how to answer everyone."

- COLOSSIANS 4:6 (NIV)

E ffective communication is essential for building strong relationships and fostering understanding within our family. It involves both listening attentively to others and expressing ourselves in a way that promotes clarity, respect, and empathy. By cultivating good communication habits, we can create an atmosphere of openness, trust, and harmony in our family.

In the Bible, we find the story of Moses as an example of the importance of communication. When God called Moses to lead the Israelites out of Egypt, Moses was hesitant and expressed his insecurities and limitations. However, God assured Moses that He would be with him and help him communicate His messages to the people. Through Moses, God communicated His laws, guidance, and promises to the Israelites, leading them on a journey of faith and transformation.

Moses' story reminds us that effective communication requires both speaking and listening. It involves expressing our thoughts and feelings honestly and respectfully, as well as taking the time to truly hear and understand others. Just as God guided Moses, He can also guide us in our communication within the family, enabling us to speak words of love, encouragement, and wisdom.

As a family, we can cultivate effective communication by creating intentional spaces for open dialogue, where each family member has an opportunity to express their thoughts, concerns, and joys. We can practice active listening, giving our full attention to one another and seeking to understand before responding. We can use words that build up and encourage, rather than tear down.

Prompts: *Share a time when effective communication helped resolve a conflict or strengthen a relationship.*

How can we improve our listening skills as a family? What can we do to ensure that everyone feels heard and understood?

Activity: Family Storytelling Night: Dedicate an evening to sharing personal stories within the family. Each family member takes turns telling a story about an important event or lesson in their life, fostering effective communication and active listening skills.

Let us pray... *Dear Heavenly Father, thank You for the gift of communication, which allows us to express ourselves and connect with one another. Help us to be mindful of the words we speak and the way we listen within our family. Guide us in using our words to build up and encourage one another, fostering understanding and love. May our communication be filled with grace, seasoned with salt, reflecting Your wisdom and love. Amen.*

32

BALANCE

FINDING HARMONY IN ALL ASPECTS OF LIFE

"There is a time for everything and a season for every activity under the heavens."

— ECCLESIASTES 3:1 (NIV)

F inding balance in life is like orchestrating a beautiful symphony. It involves harmonizing the various elements and responsibilities we encounter, such as work, family, relationships, self-care, and faith. When we strive for balance, we create space for joy, peace, and fulfillment in every aspect of our lives.

In the Bible, we are reminded that there is a time for everything. The book of Ecclesiastes teaches us that life is made up of different seasons and activities. Just as a well-composed piece of music requires the right timing and blending of instruments, our lives require intentional choices and prioritization to achieve balance.

Finding balance begins with setting priorities and understanding that not everything can be done at once. It means recognizing that our time and energy are limited resources, and we must allocate them wisely. It involves seeking God's guidance in discerning our purpose and aligning our choices with His will.

As a family, let's have balance in our time spent together and individually by establishing interests healthy routines, and boundaries. We should encourage each other to pursue passions and interests while ensuring we maintain meaningful connections with our loved ones. By prioritizing self-care and nurturing our physical, emotional, and spiritual well-being, we create a solid foundation for a balanced life.

Prompts: *What areas of life do you feel most imbalanced? How can we work together as a family to find greater harmony in those areas?*

Share examples of activities or practices that help you find balance and bring joy to your life.

Activity: Life Wheel Exercise: Draw a wheel divided into different aspects of life (e.g., family, work, hobbies, health). Family members individually rate their satisfaction in each area and discuss ways to achieve better balance and harmony among them.

Let us pray... *Dear Lord, thank You for the reminder that there is a time for everything. Help us find balance in our lives, recognizing the importance of prioritizing our time, energy, and commitments. Guide us in making choices that align with Your will and bring harmony to all aspects of our lives. May we find joy, peace, and fulfillment as we seek balance and nurture our relationships with You and one another. Amen.*

33

FAITHFULNESS

REMAINING COMMITTED TO GOD AND ONE ANOTHER

"The one who is faithful in a very little is also faithful in much."

- LUKE 16:10A (ESV)

Faithfulness is a virtue that extends beyond our relationship with God; it also encompasses our commitment to one another in the family. It involves being loyal, trustworthy, and reliable, even in the small and seemingly insignificant matters. Just as God remains faithful to us, we are called to be faithful to our loved ones.

One example of faithfulness in everyday life can be seen in the relationship between siblings. Siblings have the opportunity to practice faithfulness by being there for each other, supporting one another, and keeping their promises. When a brother or sister stands up for their sibling, defends their honor, or offers a listening ear during a difficult time, they demonstrate the power of faithfulness in action.

Consider the story of Sarah and David, two siblings who faced a challenging situation together. David, the younger brother, struggled with learning difficulties, and it often left him feeling discouraged and frustrated. Sarah, his older sister, recognized his struggles and chose to be faithful in her support. She patiently listened to him, encouraged him, and helped him find resources and strategies to overcome his difficulties. Sarah's faithfulness in being there for David not only strengthened their bond as siblings but also empowered David to persevere and achieve success in his academic journey.

In our own family, we can cultivate faithfulness by practicing active listening, being present, and following through on our commitments. We can prioritize spending quality time together, demonstrating our loyalty and love through our actions.

Prompts: *How can we demonstrate faithfulness to God and to one another in our daily lives?*

Share examples of how God has been faithful to our family, even in challenging times.

Activity: Commitment Covenant: Create a family commitment covenant where each member pledges to remain faithful to God and one another. Display the covenant in a visible place as a reminder of the family's commitment to their faith and unity.

Let us pray... *Dear Heavenly Father, thank You for Your faithfulness to us. Help us to remain faithful to You and to one another as a family. Strengthen our commitment to living out Your will and following Your teachings. May our love and faithfulness never waver, but be deeply ingrained in our hearts and actions. Guide us to be trustworthy, supportive, and loyal to each other. Amen.*

34

BODY HEALTH

THE GIFT OF HEALTH AND CARING FOR OUR BODIES

"Or do you not know that your body is a temple of the Holy Spirit within you, whom you have from God? You are not your own, for you were bought with a price. So glorify God in your body."

- I CORINTHIANS 6:19-20 (ESV)

Our bodies are precious gifts from God, and caring for them is an essential part of honoring Him. The health and well-being of our bodies directly impact our ability to serve God, fulfill our responsibilities, and enjoy life with our loved ones. As a family, we have the opportunity to embrace the gift of health and encourage one another to care for our bodies in a responsible and respectful manner.

One way to approach body health is by developing healthy habits together as a family. We can prioritize physical activity, such as going for walks, playing sports, or dancing together. Engaging in these activities not only promotes physical fitness but also strengthens our bond as a family. We can also encourage balanced nutrition by making mindful choices about the food we eat, teaching our children the importance of nourishing their bodies with wholesome and nutritious meals.

Taking care of our bodies extends beyond physical health; it also includes nurturing our mental and emotional well-being. We can prioritize rest and relaxation, creating space for quiet reflection, and fostering an environment where open communication and emotional support are encouraged. As a family, we can learn healthy ways to cope with stress, practice gratitude, and seek God's peace in times of anxiety or uncertainty.

When we care for our bodies, we honor God by acknowledging the value and purpose He has bestowed upon us. Our bodies are temples of the Holy Spirit, and by treating them with respect and care, we glorify God in every aspect of our lives.

Prompts: *How can we prioritize physical activity and make it a fun and regular part of our family routine?*

How can we encourage healthy eating habits and make nutritious choices as a family?

What are some ways we can support one another's mental and emotional well-being?

Activity: Family Fitness Challenge: Create a friendly competition among family members to encourage physical activity. Set weekly fitness goals, such as the number of steps walked, minutes of exercise, or specific workout challenges. Keep track of progress together and celebrate achievements as a family.

Let us pray... *Heavenly Father, thank You for the gift of our bodies, which are fearfully and wonderfully made. Help us to honor You by caring for our bodies, nurturing our physical, mental, and emotional health. Guide us in making wise choices, and grant us the discipline and strength to develop healthy habits as a family. May our bodies be vessels that bring glory to Your name and enable us to fulfill Your purpose for our lives. Amen.*

———◄◊►———

35

ABUNDANCE

LIVING A LIFE FULL OF ABUNDANCE OF BLESSINGS

"I came that they may have life and have it abundantly."

- JOHN 10:10 (ESV)

G od's desire for our lives is that we experience abundance in every aspect. He wants us to live a life filled with blessings, joy, and purpose. As a family, we have the opportunity to recognize and embrace the abundant blessings that surround us, cultivating a mindset of gratitude and contentment.

There are countless examples of God's abundant provision and blessings. One of these is that of the Israelites in the wilderness. As they journeyed towards the Promised Land, God provided for their every need. He miraculously supplied manna from heaven to satisfy their hunger and brought forth water from a rock to quench their thirst. Despite their challenging circumstances, God demonstrated His faithfulness and abundance in sustaining His people.

Just like the Israelites, we too can experience God's abundant blessings in our lives. It starts with a shift in our perspective and mindset. Instead of focusing on what we lack or what we desire, we can choose to recognize and appreciate the blessings that are already present in our lives. We can express gratitude for the love and support of our family, the provision of our basic needs, the beauty of creation, and the opportunities for growth and learning.

Living a life of abundance also involves being good stewards of the blessings we receive. It means using our resources, time, and talents wisely and generously to bless others. We can engage in acts of kindness, serve our community, and extend a helping hand to those in need. By sharing our abundance with others, we not only bring joy and relief to those around us but also experience the fulfillment and joy that come from giving.

As a family, we can foster an atmosphere of abundance by cultivating gratitude, celebrating even the small blessings, and acknowledging God's hand in our lives. We can encourage one another to live with open hearts, ready to receive and share the abundance of blessings that God graciously provides.

Prompts: *What are some blessings that we often overlook in our daily lives?*

In what ways can we use our resources and talents to bless others and share our abundance?

Activity: Sharing Circle: Set aside regular time as a family to gather and share stories of abundance and blessings. Each family member can take turns sharing a personal experience or moment of abundance they have recently encountered. This activity creates a space for gratitude, celebration, and the recognition of abundance in everyday life.

Let us pray... *Dear God, thank You for the abundant blessings You pour into our lives. Help us to recognize and appreciate the abundance that surrounds us, both big and small. Teach us to live with gratitude and contentment, knowing that You are the source of all good things. May we use our blessings to bless others, share our abundance, and spread Your love in the world. Amen.*

———◆◇◆———

36

HUMOR

FINDING LAUGHTER AND JOY IN EVERYDAY LIFE

"A joyful heart is good medicine."

- PROVERBS 17:22 (ESV)

L aughter has a unique way of bringing joy and lightening our hearts. It has the power to uplift our spirits, create connections, and foster a positive atmosphere within our families. In the midst of life's challenges and busyness, humor reminds us to find delight and laughter in the simple moments of everyday life.

God's creation is filled with humor and delightful surprises. From the playful antics of animals to the funny situations we encounter, God invites us to embrace laughter and enjoy the lighter side of life. In the Bible, we see examples of humor and joy, such as the laughter of Sarah when she heard she would bear a child in her old age (Genesis 18:12). God's promise brought laughter and immense joy to her heart.

Humor helps us navigate through difficult times, alleviates stress, and strengthens our relationships. It breaks down barriers, creates bonds, and brings a sense of unity within our families. Sharing a good laugh together creates lasting memories and cultivates an atmosphere of joy and positivity.

As a family, we can intentionally seek moments of humor and laughter in our daily lives. We can enjoy lighthearted jokes, share funny stories, or watch a comedy movie together. Laughter can become a powerful tool in diffusing tension, resolving conflicts, and strengthening our connections.

It is important to remember that humor should always be kind, respectful, and uplifting. We should use humor to bring joy, never at the expense of hurting or belittling others. By cultivating a culture of humor that is rooted in love and kindness, we create an environment where everyone feels valued, accepted, and free to express themselves.

Prompts: *How does humor positively impact our relationships and overall well-being? How can we incorporate more of it into our family life?*

Can you share a funny memory or story that still brings a smile to your face?

Activity: Best Dad Jokes Contest: Organize a friendly contest where family members take turns sharing their best dad jokes. The goal is to make others laugh while holding in their own laughter. If someone fails to hold their laughter, they can perform a silly and light hearted forfeit, such as singing a funny song, doing a goofy dance, eating bad-tasting food, etc. This activity encourages laughter, bonding, and the joy of sharing light hearted moments.

Let us pray... *Dear God, Thank You for the gift of laughter and humor. Help us to find joy in the simple moments of everyday life and to share laughter with one another. Teach us to use humor as a source of joy and unity, always considering the feelings of others. May our family be filled with laughter, creating an atmosphere of joy and positivity. In Jesus' name, we pray. Amen.*

37

Stewardship

Taking care of God's creation

"The earth is the Lord's, and everything in it, the world, and all who live in it."

- Psalm 24:1 (NIV)

As a family, we are called to be good stewards of God's creation. Stewardship means recognizing that everything we have comes from God and that we have a responsibility to care for and manage His gifts with wisdom and gratitude. Our stewardship extends not only to our personal belongings but also to the precious gift of the earth and its resources.

In the beginning, God entrusted Adam and Eve with the care of the Garden of Eden, symbolizing our role as caretakers of God's creation. As we look around, we witness the beauty and intricate design of nature, which reflects God's wisdom and creativity. From the vast oceans to the towering mountains, from the colorful array of flowers to the diverse species of animals, all of creation proclaims the glory of God.

Taking care of God's creation involves both conservation and responsible consumption. It means making choices that minimize harm to the environment and promote sustainability. We can reduce waste by recycling, conserving energy and water, and practicing mindful consumption. We can appreciate the beauty of nature by spending time outdoors, nurturing plants, and caring for animals.

Stewardship also extends to our relationships with others. We are called to love and respect our fellow human beings, recognizing their inherent worth and treating them with dignity. Our stewardship involves using our resources, time, and talents to serve others and make a positive impact in our communities. By practicing generosity and compassion, we become instruments of God's love in the world.

Prompts: *How can we be better stewards of God's creation in our daily lives?*

What are some ways we can reduce waste and conserve resources as a family?

Activity: Nature Scavenger Hunt: Create a list of specific natural items or features to find in your local environment (e.g., unique rocks, different types of leaves). Explore together as a family, focusing on observing and appreciating God's creation while practicing good stewardship by leaving no trace behind.

Let us pray... *Dear God, thank You for the incredible gift of creation. Help us to be faithful stewards of the earth and all that You have entrusted to us. Guide us in making choices that reflect our gratitude for Your abundant blessings. May our actions reflect Your love for the world and our commitment to care for it. In Jesus' name, we pray.*

Amen.

38

CREATIVITY

EXPRESSING OURSELVES THROUGH ART AND IMAGINATION

"In the beginning, God created the heavens and the earth."

- GENESIS 1:1 (NIV)

C reativity is a remarkable gift bestowed upon us by our Creator. Just as God brought forth beauty and wonder in the act of creation, we too can tap into our innate creativity to express ourselves, reflect the beauty of the world, and honor God through art and imagination.

God's creativity is evident in every aspect of His creation. From the vibrant colors of a sunset to the intricate patterns of a butterfly's wings, the world is filled with awe-inspiring beauty that ignites our imagination. As human beings, we are made in the image of God, and this includes the ability to create and appreciate the arts.

Artistic expression allows us to communicate thoughts, emotions, and ideas that cannot always be conveyed through words alone. It is a powerful medium through which we can connect with others, inspire change, and bring joy. Whether it's painting, sculpting, writing, dancing, or any other form of creative expression, we have the opportunity to use our unique talents to glorify God and bring beauty into the world.

Throughout the Bible, we encounter individuals who used their creativity to honor God. David expressed his deepest emotions through heartfelt psalms and music, while Bezalel and Oholiab used their craftsmanship to build the Tabernacle as an offering to God. These examples remind us that creativity can be a form of worship and a way to bring glory to God.

As a family, we can nurture and celebrate creativity by providing opportunities for artistic exploration and expression. Encourage each other to engage in various art forms, allowing the freedom to experiment, make mistakes, and grow in their abilities. Embrace a spirit of curiosity and wonder, fostering an environment where imagination can flourish.

Remember, creativity is not limited to traditional forms of art. It extends to problem-solving, critical thinking, and finding innovative solutions. Encourage each other to think outside the box, embrace new ideas, and approach challenges with a creative mindset.

Prompts: *How does creativity allow us to connect with God and express ourselves?*

How can we incorporate creativity into our family life?

Activity: Upcycling Project: Choose a household item that would typically be discarded and challenge each family member to repurpose it creatively. Provide materials and guidance as needed. Come together to showcase the transformed creations and discuss the importance of thinking outside the box and embracing creative solutions.

Let us pray... *Dear God, thank You for the gift of creativity. Help us to embrace and celebrate the unique talents You have bestowed upon each of us. May our creativity be a reflection of Your beauty and a way to honor You. Guide us as we explore different forms of artistic expression and use our creativity to bring joy, inspire change, and glorify Your name. Amen.*

39

ACCEPTANCE

EMBRACING DIFFERENCES AND DIVERSITY

"Accept one another, then, just as Christ accepted you, in order to bring praise to God."

- ROMANS 15:7 (NIV)

A cceptance is a powerful virtue that calls us to embrace the unique qualities, perspectives, and experiences of others. It is an essential ingredient for building strong relationships, fostering understanding, and creating a harmonious and inclusive environment within our families and communities.

In the Bible, we are reminded of Christ's unconditional acceptance of all people. Jesus reached out to those who were marginalized, embracing them with love, compassion, and grace. He taught us to love our neighbors as ourselves, regardless of their background, culture, or differences. Jesus set an example of acceptance that we are called to follow.

As a family, we can cultivate acceptance by celebrating diversity and embracing the unique qualities that each family member brings. We can foster an environment where everyone feels valued, respected, and included. Encourage open and honest conversations about differences, and teach children the importance of empathy, kindness, and embracing others for who they are.

Acceptance does not mean we have to agree with or endorse everything about someone. It means recognizing the inherent worth and dignity of every individual and treating them with respect, regardless of our differences. It involves listening with an open mind, seeking to understand other's perspectives, and being willing to learn from one another.

Prompts: *How can we celebrate and embrace the differences within our family? How can we extend acceptance to others outside our family?*

What are some practical ways we can demonstrate acceptance in our daily lives?

Activity: Culture Night: Have a family night dedicated to learning about and appreciating different cultures. Each family member can research a specific culture and present their findings, including traditional food, music, clothing, and customs. This activity promotes acceptance and understanding of diverse backgrounds and perspectives.

Let us pray... *Dear God, thank You for creating each of us uniquely and wonderfully. Help us to embrace and celebrate the beautiful diversity around us. Teach us to love and accept one another as Christ has accepted us. May our families be a shining example of acceptance, fostering an environment of love, respect, and understanding. Amen.*

40

REST

FINDING REJUVENATION IN SABBATH AND DOWNTIME

"Come to me, all you who are weary and burdened, and I will give you rest."

— MATTHEW 11:28 (NIV)

R est is a precious gift that allows us to rejuvenate our bodies, minds, and spirits. In the busyness of life, finding moments of rest is essential for our overall well-being. As a family, embracing the concept of rest and observing Sabbath can bring us closer to God and help us recharge.

Even God, after creating the world, rested on the seventh day, setting it apart as a day of rest and worship. God knew that we need time to pause, reflect, and replenish our energy. Resting on the Sabbath allows us to reconnect with God, find solace in His presence, and experience His peace.

Rest is not just about physical relaxation; it also involves finding balance in our lives. It means saying no to unnecessary busyness and making room for activities that bring us joy and fulfillment. Resting allows us to recharge our bodies, clear our minds, and find inspiration. It enables us to be more present and attentive to the needs of our family members, fostering deeper connections and intimacy.

As a family, we can prioritize rest by setting aside dedicated times for Sabbath and downtime. This may involve creating a peaceful atmosphere at home, engaging in activities that bring joy and relaxation, and intentionally disconnecting from the demands of work and technology. By embracing rest, we create space for reflection, quality time with loved ones, and spiritual nourishment.

In a world that glorifies busyness and productivity, rest may seem counterintuitive. However, God invites us to find rest in Him, knowing that true rejuvenation comes from being in His presence. By embracing rest, we acknowledge our dependence on God, surrender our worries and burdens to Him, and find strength in His unfailing love.

Prompts: *How can we create a restful atmosphere in our home? What activities bring us joy and relaxation?*

How can we intentionally set aside time for Sabbath and rest in our busy schedules?

Activity: Technology Detox Day: Designate a day where the family takes a break from screens and digital devices. Instead, engage in restful activities such as reading books, going for walks, doing puzzles, or having meaningful conversations. This intentional break from technology allows for rejuvenation and quality time together.

Let us pray... *Dear God, thank You for the gift of rest. Help us to prioritize rest in our lives and as a family. Teach us to find rejuvenation in Your presence and to embrace the Sabbath as a time of reflection, worship, and connection with You and one another. May our restful times bring us closer to You and strengthen our bonds as a family. Amen.*

41

SACRIFICE

PUTTING OTHERS' NEEDS BEFORE OUR OWN

"Greater love has no one than this: to lay down one's life for one's friends."

- JOHN 15:13 (NIV)

Sacrifice is a powerful expression of love that calls us to put others' needs before our own. It involves selflessness, compassion, and a willingness to give up something valuable for the well-being of others. As a family, embracing the spirit of sacrifice strengthens our relationships, fosters empathy, and reflects the love of Christ.

We all know about the ultimate sacrifice made by Jesus Christ. He willingly laid down His life on the cross to redeem humanity and reconcile us with God. Jesus taught us that sacrificial love is the greatest love of all. He modeled humility, service, and selflessness, showing us the way to love others sacrificially.

Sacrifice also involves forgiveness and reconciliation. It means letting go of grudges, extending grace, and seeking restoration in our relationships. By sacrificing our pride and ego, we pave the way for healing and growth. As we learn to forgive and make sacrifices, we reflect the love and forgiveness we have received from God.

The act of sacrifice may not always be easy, and it may require us to step out of our comfort zones or make personal sacrifices. However, when we sacrificially love others, we become channels of God's love and grace in the world. Our acts of sacrifice can inspire and impact others, creating a ripple effect of kindness and compassion.

Prompts: *How can we practice sacrificial love within our family? What are some ways we can serve and bless others in our community?*

How can sacrifice strengthen our relationships with one another and with God?

Activity: Family Giving Box: Place a box in a central location in your home and label it as the "Family Giving Box." Encourage family members to contribute items they no longer use regularly to the box with the intention of sacrificially giving to those in need. Discuss together how the contents of the box will be used to bless others, promoting a spirit of sacrifice and generosity.

Let us pray... *Dear God, thank You for the example of sacrificial love demonstrated by Jesus. Teach us to sacrificially love one another as a family. Help us to put the needs of others before our own, to extend forgiveness and grace, and to be willing to make sacrifices for the well-being of our family members and those around us. May our acts of sacrifice reflect Your love and bring glory to Your name. Amen.*

42

MINDFULNESS

LIVING IN THE PRESENT MOMENT WITH INTENTION

"This is the day the Lord has made; let us rejoice and be glad in it."

- PSALM 118:24 (NIV)

Mindfulness is the practice of intentionally being fully present in the current moment, aware of our thoughts, feelings, and surroundings. It allows us to cultivate a deep sense of gratitude, find peace in the midst of chaos, and appreciate the beauty of everyday life. As a family, embracing mindfulness enables us to connect more deeply with one another and with God's abundant blessings.

In today's fast-paced world, it's easy to get caught up in the busyness and distractions that surround us. Our minds may be occupied with worries about the future or regrets from the past, causing us to miss out on the richness of the present moment. But God calls us to be fully present and mindful of His presence in each day He has given us.

The Bible encourages us to rejoice in the day that the Lord has made. It reminds us that every moment is a precious gift from God, and we are called to embrace it with gratitude and joy. When we practice mindfulness, we cultivate a deeper appreciation for the beauty and blessings that surround us, even in the ordinary moments of life.

Being mindful also means being fully present in our interactions with one another. It involves active listening, showing genuine interest, and being aware of the needs and emotions of our family members. By practicing mindful communication, we can deepen our connections and foster a loving and supportive atmosphere within our family.

Through mindfulness, we develop an attitude of gratitude and contentment. We learn to let go of worries about the future and regrets from the past, and instead, we embrace the beauty and blessings of the present moment. Mindfulness helps us to slow down, to appreciate the little things, and to cultivate a deep sense of peace in our hearts.

Prompts: *How can we practice mindfulness in our daily lives as a family? Research some ways that work for you.*

How does mindfulness help us to connect with God and deepen our relationship with Him and each other?

Activity: Gratitude Walk: Take a family walk in a natural setting, encouraging everyone to practice mindfulness and be fully present in the moment. As you walk, each family member takes turns expressing something they are grateful for, fostering a sense of appreciation and mindfulness of the blessings around them.

Let us pray... *Dear God, thank You for the gift of each moment. Help us to be mindful of Your presence in our lives and to fully embrace the present moment with gratitude and joy. Teach us to slow down, to be aware of our thoughts and emotions, and to appreciate the blessings that surround us. May mindfulness deepen our connection with You and with one another as a family. Amen.*

43

MODESTY

VALUING INNER BEAUTY OVER EXTERNAL APPEARANCE

"Your beauty should not come from outward adornments, such as elaborate hairstyles and the wearing of gold jewelry or fine clothes. Rather, it should be that of your inner self, the unfading beauty of a gentle and quiet spirit, which is of great worth in God's sight."

- 1 PETER 3:3-4 (NIV)

Modesty is a virtue that teaches us to value inner beauty over external appearance. It encourages us to focus on our character, treating others with kindness and respect. In the Bible, we find the story of Ruth, a Moabite widow who exemplified modesty through her actions.

Ruth showed great humility and modesty as she cared for her mother-in-law, Naomi. She selflessly accompanied Naomi on their journey back to Naomi's homeland. Ruth worked diligently in the fields, quietly gleaning after the harvesters to provide for both herself and Naomi.

Ruth's modesty and hard work caught the attention of Boaz, a relative of

Naomi's deceased husband, who recognized her character and eventually married her. This story reminds us that true beauty and worth come from within, not from seeking attention or external appearances.

Let us encourage one another to embrace the virtue of modesty, valuing inner beauty over external appearances. May we strive to treat others with kindness and respect, knowing that true beauty comes from the heart.

Just as Ruth's modesty and hard work were recognized and rewarded, our acts of modesty can have a significant impact on our relationships and our journey of faith.

Prompts: *How can we cultivate modesty in our daily lives?*

How does practicing modesty contribute to our relationships and our journey of faith?

Activity: Inner Beauty Affirmations: Set aside a dedicated time each day for family members to offer sincere compliments and affirmations focused on inner qualities, character, and actions. This activity promotes a culture of valuing and appreciating inner beauty and goodness.

Let us pray... *Dear God, thank You for the example of Ruth, who demonstrated modesty and humility through her actions. Help us to embrace the virtue of modesty, valuing inner beauty over external appearances. May our words and actions reflect the beauty of our hearts and draw others closer to You. In Jesus' name, we pray. Amen.*

44

HEALTHY RELATIONSHIPS

BUILDING STRONG CONNECTIONS WITH OTHERS

"Be completely humble and gentle; be patient, bearing with one another in love."

- EPHESIANS 4:2 (NIV)

Healthy relationships are a precious treasure in our lives. They bring love, support, and joy, and they contribute to our overall well-being. As a family, building strong connections with others is an essential aspect of our journey, and it requires intentional effort and commitment.

Ephesians 4:2 reminds us of key qualities to nurture in our interactions with one another. We are encouraged to be humble, acknowledging that we are not perfect and that we can learn from one another. Gentleness and patience are essential, allowing us to approach one another with kindness and understanding. Bearing with one another in love means accepting and supporting each other, even in times of disagreement or difficulty.

Furthermore, we can look to Jesus as the ultimate example of love and healthy relationships. Jesus demonstrated humility, gentleness, and patience in His interactions with others. He embraced diversity, loved unconditionally, and prioritized the well-being of those around Him. His love was sacrificial and selfless, and He calls us to follow His example in our relationships.

As a family, we can actively work on building healthy relationships by putting these qualities into practice. We can choose to listen attentively and empathetically, seeking to understand one another's perspectives and emotions. Instead of reacting impulsively, we can respond with kindness and patience. We can offer forgiveness and extend grace, recognizing that we all make mistakes and need second chances. By nurturing healthy relationships within our family, we create a safe and loving environment where each person can grow and flourish.

Prompts: *How can we practice humility, gentleness, and patience in our relationships with one another?*

What are some ways we can actively listen and seek to understand each other better?

In what ways can we demonstrate love and acceptance, even when faced with differences or conflicts?

Activity: Family Recipe Book: Create a family recipe book that includes favorite recipes passed down through generations and new ones created by family members. Encourage each person to write a short reflection on the memories and relationships associated with their chosen recipe, emphasizing the importance of sharing meals and building strong connections.

Let us pray... *Dear God, thank You for the gift of healthy relationships. Help us to build strong connections with one another based on humility, gentleness, patience, and love. Guide us in our interactions, that we may create a loving and supportive environment within our family. Teach us to extend grace and forgiveness, to listen with empathy, and to value and appreciate one another. Amen.*

45

TRUSTING GOD'S PLAN

SURRENDERING TO HIS GUIDANCE AND TIMING

"Trust in the Lord with all your heart and lean not on your own understanding; in all your ways submit to him, and he will make your paths straight."

- PROVERBS 3:5-6 (NIV)

Trusting God's plan is an act of surrendering our own desires and understanding to His perfect wisdom and timing. It requires faith and patience as we navigate through life's uncertainties, knowing that God is in control and has a purpose for each of us. As a family, learning to trust God's plan cultivates a deep sense of peace, hope, and assurance.

Imagine your family planning a trip to a new destination. You may have certain expectations and ideas about how the trip will unfold. But often, things don't go exactly as planned. There may be unexpected detours, roadblocks, or changes in weather. In those moments, trusting the GPS or map and following its directions becomes crucial.

In the same way, trusting God's plan requires us to surrender our own understanding and rely on His guidance. It means acknowledging that

He sees the bigger picture and knows what lies ahead, even when we can't fully comprehend it. Just as you trust the GPS to lead you to your destination, trusting God's plan means allowing Him to navigate our lives and guide us along the journey.

Reflect on how God has worked in your family's life in the past. Think about moments when things seemed uncertain or didn't go according to your plans, yet God's hand was evident, leading you to a better outcome or a valuable lesson. Those experiences serve as reminders that God's plan is trustworthy and that He can turn any situation, even the challenging ones, for our good.

Prompts: *Share a time when you experienced the faithfulness of God's plan in your life.*

How can we support one another in trusting God's plan, especially during challenging times?

Activity: Letter to God: Have each family member write a letter to God, expressing their hopes, dreams, and concerns. Encourage them to surrender their desires and trust in His plan. They can choose to share excerpts from their letters, fostering open and honest conversations about trusting God's plan for their lives.

Let us pray... *Dear God, thank You for the assurance that Your plans for us are perfect. Help us to trust in Your guidance and timing, even when we don't understand or when life seems uncertain. Teach us to surrender our own desires and lean on Your wisdom, knowing that You have our best interests at heart. Strengthen our faith as a family and fill our hearts with peace, hope, and assurance. Amen.*

46

COURAGEOUS FAITH

STEPPING OUT IN TRUST AND OBEDIENCE

"Have I not commanded you? Be strong and courageous. Do not be afraid; do not be discouraged, for the Lord your God will be with you wherever you go."

—JOSHUA 1:9 (NIV)

Courageous faith is like taking a leap of trust and obedience, knowing that God is with us every step of the way. It means overcoming fear and doubts and stepping out in faith, even when the path ahead seems uncertain. As a family, cultivating courageous faith strengthens our bond with God and empowers us to face life's challenges with confidence.

Do you know the story of Esther from the Bible? She was faced with a dangerous situation where her people, the Jews, were at risk. Esther had to make a choice: to remain silent and potentially save herself or to speak up and advocate for her people, risking her own life. Esther displayed courageous faith by stepping out in obedience and trusting God's plan. As a result, her bravery saved her people from destruction.

In our own lives, courageous faith means listening to God's voice, seeking His guidance, and following His leading, even when it goes against popular opinion or requires us to face challenging circumstances. It means relying on God's strength and promises, knowing that He will equip us for the journey.

Think about a time when your family faced a decision or a situation that required courage. It could have been standing up for what is right, facing a difficult transition, or embarking on a new adventure. In those moments, it might have felt easier to stay within our comfort zone, but God calls us to step out in faith, trusting in His guidance and provision.

Prompts: *Share a time when you or someone you know demonstrated courageous faith.*

What are some practical ways we can practice courageous faith as a family, both individually and collectively?

Activity: Trust Walk: Blindfold one family member and have another guide them through an obstacle course or a safe outdoor path. This activity symbolizes the need to trust and follow God's guidance even when we can't see the way ahead.

Let us pray... *Dear God, thank You for the example of courageous faith displayed throughout the Bible. Help us to trust in Your plans and step out in obedience, even when it requires courage. Give us the strength and confidence to face the challenges that come our way, knowing that You are with us. May our family be a testament to the power of courageous faith, and may it strengthen our bond with You. Amen.*

47

CELEBRATING GOD'S CREATION

RECOGNIZING THE BEAUTY OF NATURE

"The heavens declare the glory of God; the skies proclaim the work of his hands."

- PSALM 19:1 (NIV)

Take a moment to think about the awe-inspiring beauty of nature. Whether it's the vibrant colors of a sunset, the delicate petals of a flower, or the majestic mountains, God's creation surrounds us with signs of His glory. Through nature, we catch a glimpse of His power, wisdom, and infinite love.

Celebrating God's creation is an opportunity for our family to recognize and appreciate the beauty and wonder of the natural world around us. It is a reminder of God's creativity and His loving care for every detail of His creation. By cultivating a deep appreciation for nature, we can draw closer to God and develop a sense of stewardship for the earth He has entrusted to us.

Spending time outdoors, exploring, and observing the natural world with your family is an invaluable experience. Take walks in the park, visit botanical gardens, or plan camping trips where you can immerse yourselves in the wonders of creation. Encourage each family member to engage their senses, marvel at the intricate details, and reflect on the Creator behind it all.

You can also study God's Word together and discover the many references to nature found throughout the Bible. From the vastness of the ocean to the birds of the air, Scripture is filled with poetic descriptions of God's creation. Reflect on these passages and discuss how they deepen your appreciation for the world around you.

Prompts: *Brainstorm ways in which we can be good stewards of the environment and make a positive impact on the earth.*

Share some of your favorite experiences in nature and if they have impacted your faith journey.

Activity: Nature Photography Expedition: Go on a family photography expedition to capture the beauty of God's creation. Each family member can use their smartphone or a camera to take pictures of interesting landscapes, animals, or plants. Compile the photos into a digital album or create a family scrapbook.

Let us pray... *Dear God, thank You for the beauty and wonder of Your creation. Help us to recognize and celebrate the work of Your hands all around us. Open our eyes to the intricate details and the breathtaking landscapes that point to Your glory. May our family be good stewards of the earth and develop a deep sense of awe and gratitude for Your creation. Amen.*

48

GOD'S PROVISION

TRUSTING IN HIS ABUNDANT BLESSINGS

"And my God will meet all your needs according to the riches of his glory in Christ Jesus."

- PHILIPPIANS 4:19 (NIV)

Reflect on the many ways God has provided for your family. Whether it's the roof over your head, the food on your table, or the relationships you cherish. God's provision is a testament to His faithfulness and His abundant blessings in our lives. It is a reminder that we can trust Him to meet our needs, both spiritual and physical. As a family, cultivating a heart of gratitude and trusting in God's provision helps us develop a deep sense of contentment and reliance on Him.

In the Bible, we find countless stories of God's provision. One example is the story of the Israelites in the wilderness. God sustained them with manna from heaven and water from a rock, providing for their physical needs day after day. This story reminds us that just as God faithfully provided for His people in the past, He will continue to provide for us today.

Trusting in God's provision involves surrendering our worries and anxieties to Him. It means recognizing that He knows our needs and is faithful to supply them in His perfect timing and in ways that are best for us. When we trust in God's provision, we can experience peace and contentment, knowing that He is in control.

Take time to express gratitude as a family, acknowledging His faithfulness and goodness.

God's provision is not only for our benefit but also for us to share with others. Engage in acts of kindness and service as a family, whether through volunteering, donating to those in need, or simply reaching out to someone who could use a helping hand.

Prompts: *Reflect on Philippians 4:19. How does this verse encourage us to trust in God's provision?*

Share moments when you have experienced God's provision in your lives. How did it impact your faith?

Activity: Family Bake Sale for Charity: Plan and organize a family bake sale to raise funds for a charitable cause or organization. Involve each family member in the process, from brainstorming and baking to setting up the sale. Discuss the blessings of being able to give and the impact of God's provision in our lives.

Let us pray... *Dear God, thank You for Your abundant blessings and faithful provision in our lives. Help us to trust in Your provision and cultivate hearts of gratitude. Teach us to rely on You for all our needs, both spiritual and physical. Guide us in sharing Your blessings with others and being generous with what You have entrusted to us. Amen.*

49

LETTING GO OF WORRY

FINDING PEACE IN GOD'S CARE

"Therefore I tell you, do not worry about your life, what you will eat or drink; or about your body, what you will wear. Is not life more than food, and the body more than clothes?"

- MATTHEW 6:25 (NIV)

Worry is a common struggle that many of us face, but as a family, we can learn to let go of worry and find peace in God's care. Worry can consume our thoughts, steal our joy, and hinder our ability to fully trust in God. However, when we choose to surrender our worries to Him, we can experience the peace that surpasses all understanding.

In Matthew 6:25, Jesus reminds us not to worry about the basic necessities of life. He points out that God takes care of the birds of the air and the flowers of the field, and if He provides for them, how much more will He provide for us, His beloved children? This passage serves as a gentle reminder that God is aware of our needs and that He is faithful to care for us.

As a family, we can practice letting go of worry by bringing our concerns to God in prayer. Encourage each family member to share their worries and fears, and pray together, asking God for His guidance and peace. God is your loving Father who listens to your prayers and is always present to comfort and provide for them.

Encourage open communication within the family, creating a safe space where everyone feels heard and understood. Encourage each family member to share their worries and concerns, and actively listen with empathy and support. Remind one another of God's faithfulness and how He has carried you through difficult times in the past.

Prompts: *Share some of the worries you have experienced and how you have found peace in God's care.*

Discuss practical ways to shift our focus from worry to gratitude in our daily lives.

Reflect on Matthew 6:25. What does this verse teach us about God's care for us?

Activity: Bubble Release: Give each family member a small bottle of bubbles. Go to an open outdoor space and release the worries by blowing bubbles into the air. As the bubbles float away, encourage the family to visualize their worries being lifted and released, finding peace in God's loving care.

Let us pray... *Dear God, thank You for Your loving care and faithfulness in our lives. Help us to surrender our worries to You and find peace in Your care. Teach us to trust in Your provision and have faith in Your guiding hand. Give us grateful hearts and the ability to shift our focus from worry to gratitude. May Your peace guard our hearts and minds. Amen.*

50

CULTIVATING A HEART OF WORSHIP

HONORING GOD THROUGH PRAISE AND ADORATION

"Shout for joy to the Lord, all the earth. Worship the Lord with gladness; come before him with joyful songs."

- PSALM 100:1-2 (NIV)

Cultivating a heart of worship is about honoring God through praise, adoration, and gratitude. It is an expression of our love for Him and a recognition of His greatness, goodness, and faithfulness. As a family, when we engage in worship together, we create a sacred space where we can draw closer to God and experience His presence.

In Psalm 100:1-2, we are called to shout for joy and worship the Lord with gladness. This psalm reminds us that worship is not just an individual act but a collective experience that involves all the earth. It invites us to come before God with joyful songs, expressing our heartfelt gratitude and awe for who He is and what He has done.

Explore different forms of worship, such as reading Scripture aloud, praying together, and creating artwork or crafts that reflect your adoration for God. Engage all your senses in worship, whether it's lighting candles, creating a prayer corner, or using essential oils or incense to create a worshipful atmosphere.

Encourage each family member to share something they are grateful for during your times of worship. It could be a specific blessing, an answered prayer, or simply the gift of being together as a family. Expressing gratitude shifts our focus from our own needs and concerns to God's goodness and provision.

As you gather for worship, encourage a spirit of reverence and awe. Create a space that is free from distractions, where you can fully focus on God. Reflect on His character and encourage each other to share how they have experienced God's faithfulness, love, and grace in their lives. This will deepen your understanding and appreciation of who God is.

Prompts: *How does worship deepen our connection with God and strengthen our faith?*

Share a song or worship experience that has had a meaningful impact on you.

Discuss different ways we can incorporate worship into our daily lives.

Activity: Family Worship Night: Set aside a special evening for a family worship night. Choose your favorite worship songs, sing together, and express gratitude to God through heartfelt prayers. Encourage family members to share personal reflections on how they have experienced God's presence and faithfulness. Create artwork to express their worship and adoration for God and the family he's provided them with.

Let us pray... *Dear God, we come before You with hearts filled with praise and adoration. Thank You for who You are and for Your faithfulness in our lives. Help us to cultivate a heart of worship, to honor You with gladness and joy. Open our hearts to experience Your presence as we lift up our voices in praise. May our worship draw us closer to You and deepen our love for You. Amen.*

51

FAMILY LEGACY

A REPRESENTATION OF YOUR FAMILY'S HISTORY AND
THE COLLECTIVE JOURNEY YOU'RE ON TOGETHER

*"But from everlasting to everlasting the Lord's love is with those who fear
him, and his righteousness with their children's children."*

- PSALM 103:17 (NIV)

F amily legacy is a precious gift that we pass on from one generation
to another. It is a representation of our family's history, values, and
the collective journey we embark on together. As a family, we have the
opportunity to create a legacy that reflects God's love, faithfulness, and
righteousness.

In the Bible, we find numerous stories that highlight the importance of
family legacy. One such story is that of Abraham. God called Abraham
to leave his homeland and promised to make him the father of many
nations. Despite facing challenges and setbacks, Abraham remained
faithful to God's promise, and his legacy became a testament to God's
faithfulness for generations to come.

Abraham's story teaches us the significance of obedience, trust, and passing on our faith to future generations. As a family, we can look to Abraham's example and embrace our role in building a legacy that honors God.

To begin creating a family legacy, we can start by exploring our family's history. Share stories of our ancestors, their experiences, and the values they cherished & reflect on how their journey has shaped who we are as a family today.

Discuss the values and principles that are important to our family. Identify the virtues and qualities that we want to pass on to future generations. These can include love, compassion, forgiveness, integrity, and a heart for serving others. Encourage each family member to contribute their thoughts and ideas.

Furthermore, try to engage in meaningful traditions that strengthen family bonds and reinforce the values we hold dear. This can include regular family meals, celebrations of significant milestones, and volunteering together in service projects. These shared experiences create lasting memories and reinforce the importance of family unity. Our actions speak louder than words, and by living out our faith, integrity, and love, we inspire the next generation to do the same.

Family legacy is not something that is built overnight but is a lifelong journey.

Prompts: *What are some of the values and principles that are important to our family?*

Share stories of our ancestors and discuss how their experiences have influenced our family's journey.

Reflect on Psalm 103:17. How does God's love and righteousness extend to future generations?

Activity: Time Capsule: Create a family time capsule by gathering meaningful items or mementos that represent the current phase of life. Seal the items in a container and choose a date in the future to open it. Discuss the significance of new beginnings and the anticipation of what the future holds.

Let us pray... *Dear Heavenly Father, thank You for the gift of family and the opportunity to build a legacy that reflects Your love and faithfulness. Guide us as we seek to create a family legacy that honors You. Help us to pass on our values, faith, and love for You to future generations. May our family be a testament to Your goodness and righteousness. In Jesus' name, we pray. Amen.*

NEW BEGINNINGS

STARTING AFRESH WITH HOPE AND RENEWAL

"Therefore, if anyone is in Christ, the new creation has come: The old has gone, the new is here!"

- 2 CORINTHIANS 5:17 (NIV)

New beginnings bring a sense of hope, renewal, and opportunity. They allow us to leave behind the past and embrace a fresh start. As a family, we have the chance to experience new beginnings together and witness God's transformative power in our lives.

In the Bible, we find stories of individuals who experienced remarkable new beginnings through their encounters with God. One such story is that of the prodigal son. This young man made poor choices, squandered his inheritance, and found himself living in despair. However, when he realized the error of his ways and humbly returned to his father, he was welcomed with open arms and given a new beginning. His father's love and forgiveness transformed his life and restored him to a place of honor.

The prodigal son's story reminds us that no matter our past mistakes or failures, God offers us the opportunity for a new beginning. Through

His love and grace, He invites us to leave behind our old ways and embrace a fresh start in Him. We can experience His forgiveness, restoration, and transformation.

To embark on a new beginning as a family, we can:

1. Seek God's guidance: Through prayer and seeking His Word, we can find direction and wisdom for the new season ahead. Invite God to lead and guide us as a family, trusting in His plans and purposes.

2. Let go of the past: Leave behind past hurts, mistakes, and regrets. Embrace forgiveness and release any burdens that weigh us down. Allow God's grace to heal and restore our hearts, individually and collectively.

3. Set goals and aspirations: Together, as a family, identify goals, dreams, and aspirations for the future. Encourage one another to pursue personal growth, development, and the fulfillment of God-given talents and passions.

4. Embrace change: Be open to change and embrace the opportunities it presents. Adjusting to new routines, environments, or dynamics may require flexibility and a willingness to adapt. Trust that God is with us in the midst of change and that He is working for our good.

5. Encourage one another: Offer support, encouragement, and accountability as we navigate new beginnings. Celebrate each family member's progress and milestones along the way. Let love, grace, and kindness be the foundation of our interactions.

6. Trust in God's provision: Have faith that God will provide for our needs as we step into new beginnings. Trust in His timing and believe that He has good plans for our family's future.

New beginnings can be both exciting and challenging, but with God at the center, and family by our sides, we can confidently step forward in hope and renewal. Let us embrace the opportunity to start afresh, trusting in God's faithfulness and the transformation He brings into our lives.

Prompts: *Share a time when you experienced a new beginning. How did it impact your life?*

What are some goals or dreams you have for our family's new beginning?

How can we support and encourage one another during times of change and new beginnings?

Activity: Renewal Ritual: Choose a symbol of new beginnings, such as planting seeds or lighting a candle. As a family, engage in a meaningful ritual to signify letting go of the past and embracing fresh starts. Reflect on the hope and possibilities that come with new beginnings.

Let us pray... *Dear Heavenly Father, thank You for the gift of new beginnings. We surrender our lives and our family into Your hands, trusting in Your faithfulness and guidance. As we embark on this new season, fill us with hope and renewal. Help us to embrace the opportunities that come our way, knowing that You are with us every step of the journey. May Your love and grace be evident in our family's story. In Jesus' name, we pray. Amen.*

AFTERWORD

Congratulations on completing this family devotional! I genuinely hope that it has been a valuable companion on your journey of faith. As you look back on the pages you've read, I encourage you to pause and reflect on the lessons learned, the wisdom gained, and the growth experienced by each member of your family.

Remember, this devotional is just the beginning of a lifelong adventure in growing closer to God as a family. The insights and teachings you have encountered within these pages will serve as a foundation for your future endeavors. Embrace the opportunities and challenges that lie ahead, knowing that you are equipped with the tools to navigate them with confidence and purpose.

I want to express my deepest gratitude to you for choosing this book and allowing me to be a part of your family's spiritual journey. As an author, every reader's support means the world to me. Your engagement with the content and your willingness to learn and grow reaffirm my purpose in sharing these words.

If you found this family devotional book valuable and impactful, I kindly ask for your support by leaving a review. Reviews play a crucial role in helping authors like myself reach a wider audience. Your honest review will not only make my day but also contribute to the growth of this book and future projects, as well as assist other families seeking to strengthen their bond with God.

You can easily leave a review by scanning the QR code below or by searching for "Biblical Teachings" on Amazon. Additionally, I invite you to explore my other books, where you can find further insights and teachings to deepen your family's faith and personal growth.

Customer reviews
★★★★☆ 4.6 out of 5

Review this product
Share your thoughts with other customers

Write a customer review

Once again, thank you for your readership and for journeying through this family devotional book. May your shared faith continue to flourish, bringing your family closer together and closer to God's love and grace.

Made in United States
Troutdale, OR
10/29/2024